How To Publish a Book & Sell a Million Copies

Ted Nicholas

Enterprise · Dearborn

a division of Dearborn Publishing Group, Inc.

While a great deal of care has been taken to provide accurate and current information, the ideas, suggestions, general principles and conclusions presented in this text are subject to local, state and federal laws and regulations, court cases and any revisions of same. The reader is thus urged to consult legal counsel regarding any points of law—this publication should not be used as a substitute for competent legal advice.

© 1975, 1980, 1993 by Ted Nicholas

Published by Enterprise • Dearborn
a division of Dearborn Publishing Group, Inc.

For mail orders, write: Nicholas Direct, Inc., 19918 Gulf Blvd. #7, Indian Shores, FL 34635. Telephone: 813-596-4966, Fax: 813-596-6900.

Printed in the United States of America

93 94 95 10 9 8 7 6 5 4 3 2 1

Library of Congress Cataloging-in-Publication Data

Nicholas, Ted, 1934–
     How to publish a book and sell a million copies / Ted Nicholas.
          p.   cm.
     Rev. ed. of: How to self-publish your own book & make it a bestseller. Rev. 1980
     Includes bibliographical references and index.
     ISBN 0-79310-620-6
     1. Self-publishing—United States.   I. Nicholas, Ted, 1934– How to self-publish your own book & make it a bestseller.   II. Title.
     Z285.5.N53   1993
     070.5'93—dc20
                                                                                   93-13030
                                                                                        CIP

Dedication

Perhaps the most precious and important right of all free people is freedom of speech. In America we are guaranteed this right under the First Amendment of the Constitution.

In dictatorships it is no accident that as soon as leaders assume power, one of their first acts is to take away the citizens' freedom of expression. Censorship and control of the printing presses are sought by all despots.

This book is dedicated to the real unsung heroes of all human societies—the writers and publishers who, through their efforts, keep everyone free.

Acknowledgments

I love books. Being self-educated, I have discovered them to be the most important intellectual influence in my life.

My sincere thanks to all the hundreds of authors too numerous to mention who helped me, through their books, build my base of knowledge and awareness.

Here's what others just like you have said about *How To Publish a Book and Sell a Million Copies*:

> *"Expert priceless advice from the world's most successful self-publisher. Get thousands of tested marketing and self-publishing ideas worth millions of dollars in your mailbox. Owning* How To Publish a Book and Sell a Million Copies *will give you over 20 years of proven shortcuts for mail order marketing information products—including newsletters, Special Reports, audio tapes, videos, books and disks. At $1,000 a copy, this book would be a steal!"*
>
> **Andrew S. Linick, PhD——The Copyologist** ®
> **Direct Response Marketing & Publishing Consultant**
> **Author,** *Secrets of a Mail Order Fortunaire*™

> *"*How To Publish a Book and Sell a Million Copies *takes the mystery out of marketing. This book can make the difference between success or failure. Yes! We also reduced our advertising costs by 25 percent for the same space!"*
>
> **Dr. Tag Powell**
> **Top of the Mountain Publishing**

> *"Superb! I was pleased to get more than I expected from your book. You've really spilled the beans on the self-publishing business!"*
>
> **Margaret Barnes**
> **Denver, Colorado**

"Thank you so much for all the invaluable information and knowledge you shared in your book, How To Publish a Book and Sell a Million Copies. *We were amazed by all the inside secrets and techniques that you unselfishly revealed."*

Jim and Vickie Feutz
Suncoast Pension Group
Tampa, Florida

"The information in your book is priceless. I do know that anybody seriously entertaining the idea of self-publishing a book, or in fact, anybody in the business, must have your book or attend your seminar."

Dr. Joachim DePosada
Miami, Florida

*"*How To Publish a Book and Sell a Million Copies *is a gem! The information is truly top secret, and in the right hands, worth millions of dollars! Thank you. Your book reveals the most valuable information for writers and entrepreneurs in the world today!"*

Blade Thomas
Malibu, California

"Thanks for the guidance and suggestions during my writing of several bestsellers."

Doug Casey
Author, *Crisis Investing*

"As a beginner in the self-publishing and direct selling industries, I found your book extremely educational and informative as well as motivational. Additionally, it was important that the information came from years of experience rather than textbook theory."

Norman Caldwell
Bradenton, Florida

"How To Publish a Book and Sell a Million Copies has been a great investment. I have learned more about selling books and videos through the methods explained in your book than I learned in the previous three years of constant research. Thank you!"

Royal Edwards
Merrimack, New Hampshire

"I learned more usable techniques for headline selection, ad format, rate negotiation and ad placement of display advertising with your book than I could have learned in a lifetime of trial and error. Thanks!"

Pat McAllister
The Information Exchange
Carbondale, Colorado

Contents

Note:

All of the publishing and marketing strategies and techniques in this book apply equally to all information products. This includes books, Special Reports, newsletters, computer disks, audio and video tapes.

However, for the sake of simplicity and to avoid duplication, I will use the word "books" for the most part or "your product" when I'm discussing any information product.

Introduction

As an entrepreneur or author interested in seeing your book "in print" (or newsletter, Special Report, or audio or video tape, etc.), you have knocked on the door of one of the most glamorous yet mysterious institutions in this country: the publishing industry.

The mystery is really no accident, and most authors haven't a clue as to the "ins" of publishing, nor what actually happens within the sacred walls of a publishing house. It is a well-kept secret, and only a person who has been in the inside can ever give a true picture of what it's all about.

You as Publisher

The purpose of this book is to show you what is involved in publishing. It will take you inside, introduce you to the terminology, methodology and the techniques of publishing. It will give you the facts so that you will be well prepared for your future as a publisher. You alone will have control over the work. Not a word or a comma will be changed by anyone but you. You will be the only one responsible for its success or failure. That kind of power is hard to come by.

More important, as an author who has published 52 books as well as newsletters, Special Reports, video tapes, audio tapes, computer disks, seminars, etc. and has sold over 2.5 million copies, I will explain the complete process from manuscript to bestseller in terms any layperson will be able to understand.

I was not born into a publishing family. I learned it. And through this book, I will demonstrate to you every technique necessary to publishing, as well as the essentials of advertising and promotion. These last two are vitally necessary to make your product a bestselling success.

Myths about Publishing

There are several myths about publishing that I would like to dispel at the outset. Until I published my own work, I thought the "Bible" of the publishing world was reflected in the bestseller lists. Actually, these lists have little to do with the number of books sold in the United States. They reflect only those books sold in bookstores.

You may say to yourself that this makes sense, but can you imagine the consequences of an author's book being out-of-stock in several major bookstores? That book will slide down the charts into oblivion. The publishers will watch its downward progression and will surmise that it has run its course and stop promoting it. Where does that leave the author?

My book, *How To Form Your Own Corporation Without a Lawyer for under $75*, has been among the top 10 nonfiction bestsellers in the United States for over 20 years, but it has never appeared on a bestseller list. The reason for this is that, as stated before, the lists are compiled from information supplied by a few major bookstores. My products are sold primarily through the mail. Only about 10 percent of the total number of copies sold have been through bookstores.

Taking it a step further, nationally, 50 percent of all books sold are sold through the mail. You can readily see that an entire 50 percent----HALF!----of all the books sold in this country are not even considered on bestseller lists.

Naturally, having a book on the bestseller list is good publicity. Lots of people buy books simply because they're listed. But marketing a book or other information product through bookstores can be an expensive and time-consuming process. There are easier, more direct ways to do it, and this book shows you how.

Some other popular myths about the publishing industry include:

Myth #1—*Writing the book (or other product) is 90 percent of the task. After that's done, you can relax and watch the receipts roll in.*

False! At most, the production of any information product is only 10 percent of the whole process. Indeed, it is more involved than you think to produce a product, but it is also one of the easiest steps. Prior to its printing, your production is a creative, artistic embryo. Once it is off the press, it becomes a **product** just like light bulbs and rubber tires. Unless you want copies of your products for no other reason than to give as presents to friends and relatives, or to sit and gather dust in your basement, your product must be treated as an item that must be sold to the public.

There are literally thousands of products on a variety of important subjects that are just sitting in warehouses simply because the sales efforts were inadequate or totally nonexistent. For that very reason, a large portion of this book is devoted to promotion and sales.

Myth #2—*It costs many thousands of dollars to publish a product.*

False again. I'm going to show you how to do it in manageable steps for less than $3,000, whereby your book can cost as little as $2 or $3 a copy to print. Your audio tape or computer disk can cost less than $1—your video tape less than $8.

Myth #3—*A good product will simply "take off" once it's published, and very little will have to be spent on advertising and publicity.*

This one couldn't be further from the truth. Although the big publishing companies have millions of dollars available for advertising, this book will show you how to handle this vitally important area for less money than you would think. There are many areas in which you can get free advertising, and these will be explained. The secret lies in using low-cost classified advertisements in the beginning and selecting the media carefully. You will be shown how to choose these publications, how to write your advertisements and when to place them.

Myth #4—*Television and radio are expensive media on which you see few advertisements for information products.*

You've probably seen or heard more advertisements for information products than for any other product, almost. Talk shows are the vehicle for promoting books, and hardly a day goes by when an author isn't appearing on one of the talk shows with his or her brand-new book in hand. Radio and television are two of the **cheapest** vehicles with which to get publicity for your book. More about this later.

Myth #5—*No one is ever going to go out of their way to promote your product in times like this.*

Happily, this one is also false. The minute one person reviews your book and the review appears in print, you have some great free advertising which can be capitalized upon. In your ads, you can then say, "Reviewed by the *Los Angeles Times*, who said . . . ." At that point, others are promoting you without your having to lift a finger.

If you approach the subject of self-publishing as a series of well-formulated steps that can be accomplished without too much effort, one of the rewards could be a conventional publisher approaching you. They may ask to pick up rights to your book, offering you an attractive proposal.

Does that sound like a long shot? Well, it happened to me! But for economic as well as personal reasons, the decision was made to self-publish all of my books. The sense of control is attractive, and it is not surprising that the greater potential for profit through self-publishing is appealing as well. You can realize this too.

Your reasons for wanting a book published with your name on it can be one of many. For doctors, lawyers, professors and others, having a book published helps enhance their professional status. With many college professors, the adage "publish or perish" is heard all too often. For business people, it can pave the way to greater recognition and promotions. Other authors want to realize financial success through their literary efforts. Still others enjoy the lifestyle that being a successful publisher makes possible.

Too many writers want only to see their books in print. It is certainly a thrill to see their names on the covers. These people are not at all interested in the business side of publishing. That is their choice, of course. But to see your book become a great success, to see that it is helping many thousands of people and to enjoy a lifestyle on a higher level than you knew previously----that's the greatest thrill of all! You won't experience that kind of exhilaration if your books are lying in cold storage and no one is reading them.

The conventional publishing route is simply not open to the majority of writers, especially new ones. It is becoming more and more difficult to even get an editor interested enough to look at your manuscript, much less see the day when it rolls off the presses. There are two alternatives to the author who has a drive to see his or her book published. One is self-publishing, and the other is through a vanity press.

Subsidy, or vanity presses, will be discussed later in this book, and you will see why I believe that the most sensible and attractive option for an author is self-publishing. It is the only way to go, in my opinion. I hope that through this book, where you can see how I did it, you will come to the same conclusion.

If you plan to prepare a marketable book, there will be facts, ideas and proven methods to put you on the path of accomplishment, fame and financial rewards. Some of you will become wealthy. Others, who simply want to see their books in print, will be able to do so at minimum cost.

This book offers you an alternative that makes it possible for you to accomplish what may very well be impossible through any other channel----your own self-published bestseller!

Questions and Answers about Self-Publishing

Can the average person successfully self-publish a book?

Absolutely. There isn't really any mystery involved, nor does self-publishing require an enormous amount of money. All that's required is an interesting subject and the proper presentation.

How much of an investment will I have to make?

It depends on the length of your book, whether it is typeset by a professional, the method of printing, the size of the first printing and the quality of the paper and binding. With all of these variables, it would be impossible to give you a definite figure, but I believe self-publishing can be (and is) much less expensive than most people have believed it to be. Some self-publishers have spent less than $2,000 on their books and initial marketing.

What is the secret of success in self-publishing?

Marketing and advertising. You can write the greatest book the world has ever known, but if it doesn't reach the public, it cannot become a success.

Can I compete with the "big guys"?

Yes. And it is easier than you think. Since you are interested in only one product, you can afford to give it the time, attention and effort that large conventional publishers can't give each one of their books.

Can my book really be successful if I self-publish it?

Yes, if you go about it the right way. Many books which have been self-published have become bestsellers recently. I believe that we will be seeing more and more of this in the coming years, because it allows the author to retain more control of his or her own work. It is easier in many ways than conventional publishing. And it is more cost-effective if handled properly.

What is the difference between self-publishing and vanity presses?

Vanity presses "publish" your book by signing you to a contract (where you pay all production costs), having your book typeset and printed and often selling your books back to you. Self-publishing involves YOU having your book typeset (if desired) and printed, YOU advertising and marketing it and YOU collecting all the profits.

Will conventional publishers be interested in my books when I self-publish them?

Often it is the best route to their door. After self-publishing my first book, several publishers contacted me offering to buy reprint and paperback rights. If this is what you are interested in, self-publishing is an effective way to get their attention. But I found that self-publishing was far more profitable for me than signing with a conventional publisher on a royalty arrangement.

Don't you have to take all the risk when you self-publish? What if the book is a flop?

Yes, the self-publisher takes all the risk. If the book is well conceived and does not sell well, nine times out of ten it has not been given adequate exposure. But on the other hand, if the book is a success, you do not have to share your profits with anyone else. The key to success is marketing and advertising a self-published book.

What are the basic steps to self-publishing?

Writing the manuscript, preparing it to be printed, getting it printed, advertising the book, distributing the book, recordkeeping and----of course----counting the profits.

How many copies should I have printed?

That depends on a number of things: subject, size of the potential audience and your available funds. Usually, self-publishers start with a small first printing and use the majority of available funds for aggressive advertising efforts. You can always go to another printing when the book begins to sell. If the book doesn't sell, you haven't tied up your money in extra copies. Your money is available for more advertising.

It's also a good idea to do a small first printing because any errors can be corrected and/or changes easily can be made prior to the second printing.

I'm a college student with very little income. Would it be feasible for me to self-publish a book?

Yes. There are methods for people with limited funds to use explained in this book. You will have to have **some** working capital but not a great amount. Some capital-raising methods will also be explained.

What types of self-published books have the best chance of success?

Nonfiction products that fill needs or wants. Subjects with mass appeal----those written in clear language about understandable topics and those offering concrete information that people cannot find anywhere else. Self-help books are the most popular.

What about novels?

Novels are just as simple to get into print as nonfiction. They are different from self-help and other nonfiction books in that the market can sometimes be harder to define. However, the techniques in this book will help you toward a self-published novel.

Will reviewers review self-published books in print?

Yes. While most reviewers will not even look at a book from a vanity press, it is relatively easy for self-published authors to get their books reviewed. This includes reviews in major national publications.

What kind of outside help will I need and have to pay for?

You will need a printer. Beyond that, with the help of desktop publishing equipment, if you are able to communicate effectively in writing, if you have organized your manuscript into a cohesive unit, if you know how to proofread and if you are willing to do your advertising and public relations correctly, you will not need anyone else. And you can recognize great economies. If you would feel more comfortable, you can engage outside help in the way of editors, proofreaders or advertising professionals.

How can I advertise my book? I've heard about the thousands of dollars magazine advertisements cost.

The key to wise investments in advertising is in starting out with small, inexpensive ads and going up from there. Often, you can use inexpensive classified ads as I did when I started.

If the book sales soar, what can I expect?

a. If you are promoting your book as an additional source of income to your present job, you will have the money to continue marketing your book for even higher profits.

b. You will have the enviable freedom that only owning your own business can allow.

c. You do not have to split your profits with anyone since you are working for yourself. Therefore, the more effort you put into your business, the more money you'll earn.

d. As long as you continue to market your book, you'll have job security and the freedom to operate your business from whatever location you choose.

e. You will have the opportunity to meet people in the media as well as the publishing world if you desire.

How do I get started?
You turn the page.

Chapter 1

Your Options in Publishing

On any given day in New York City, an estimated 200,000 manuscripts sit in the files of various publishers or on the desks of their editors. With 600,000 books submitted every year, and only 70,000 actually published, the odds of an unknown writer's first book seeing the light of day at a conventional publishing house are extremely low.

Out of the books which are published, 90 percent of them do not sell out of their first printing. The average number of books in an initial printing is generally in the region of 5,000 to 10,000 copies, and many sell only a fraction of that. Neither the writer (who usually receives a royalty of between 5 and 15 percent) nor the publisher earns much money on these ventures or gains much notice, whichever is the goal.

There are notable exceptions to this rather dismal state of affairs. Some books seem to become overnight bestsellers, and the news media are filled with gossipy items about how much the movie rights are selling for and the intrigue of formal negotiations. But you can bet that these types of phenomenal successes are not accidents. It took intelligent planning by the editorial and marketing departments to get the book into the public eye in the first place.

Your Odds of Being Published

From your point of view as a writer who may not be well-known throughout the country, the odds of your book being published are ten to one against you. Above and beyond that, the odds are also ten to one against your book selling out of the first printing. And the odds are infinitesimally small that you will sell the tens of thousands of copies necessary to earn the distinction of "bestseller."

Looking at these odds can be very discouraging to the person who has writing aspirations. Often it takes months (and sometimes years) of effort to write a book. Then, when it is rejected time and time again by publishers, or when it is handled poorly by a publisher, it is an anguishing experience.

Conventional (or "risk") publishers are in business to make money. To break even on a book, a large publisher must sell a minimum of 5,000 to 10,000 copies. In order to reduce their risks, these large publishing houses seek out well-known authors. These are writers who have had books published before which were good sellers, and who have a following of people who will probably buy another book by the same author. The publishers then invest their promotion and advertising dollars to virtually guarantee profitable sales.

Even with all that working for them, in very few cases do hardcover books sell beyond 20,000 copies. Publishers hope to make their largest profits in reprints, later acquisitions by book clubs and finally through the transition to a low-cost paperback. Sometimes, there are also movie, serial, TV, and overseas rights which can be negotiated, depending upon the book.

What Conventional Publishers Can and Cannot Do

It is very surprising that large publishers seldom expend more than $50,000 in advertising and promotion, even for a bestseller. In one year my company spent in excess of $750,000 in advertising

2

my first book. The best part is that it was accomplished with little risk, on a pay-as-you-go basis.

Large publishers cannot operate like my publishing company could. But I think it is a mistake to invest so little in a book which can earn so much. Conventional publishers will grudgingly spend only the bare minimum to announce a new book; then if it doesn't sell, all further efforts are dropped. I think you can imagine the number of good books which have virtually disappeared simply because they lacked a solid marketing and advertising plan.

It is a fact that unknown authors are largely ignored by conventional publishers regardless of the quality of their books. One way around this problem is to self-publish, self-promote and create a product which will be sought out by conventional publishers, if this is your aim.

How To Form Your Own Corporation Without a Lawyer for under $75 was sent around to 12 publishers before I decided to publish it myself. It was turned down. No one was interested----mainly because they'd never heard of me.

It was a completely different story, however, after I had printed, promoted and advertised the book and had sold over 100,000 copies. Six major conventional publishers approached me with offers to buy rights to this title.

You might think that I would have been overjoyed at the thought of being published by a major publisher. Many people would be. But I wasn't. Through all the hands-on experience I had gained through self-publishing my own book, I decided that I would be far better off financially if I continued my self-publishing efforts. There was no incentive for me to share my profits with anyone else, especially since the book was so successful. I was fortunate to realize early in my publishing career that no one is as interested in your work as you are.

Even if your ultimate goal is to be published by a large conventional publisher, the self-publishing approach is recommended for your first book. Once it is successful and you are recognized within the industry, getting your second book into print through a major publishing house will be much easier. I chose to do it differently. But you may prefer to have future books published by someone else.

Promoting Your Self-Published Book

Some authors feel reluctant about promoting their own books. Many writers simply do not become involved, perhaps mostly due to lack of information as to how to do it. What they lose in the process is their greatest chance at success.

One writer (a prominent judge) recounted his experiences with his first book, which was placed with a conventional publisher. In my opinion it was an exceptionally well-written and exciting book. It was published by one of the largest and best-known publishers in the country. After two years of unimpressive sales, he visited the headquarters to learn what was being done to promote the book. He asked to see his file.

To his utter astonishment, they had never done any promotion, so there wasn't any such file! Needless to say, he is not interested in having them publish his next book.

Of course, all writers do not have unsatisfactory relationships with their publishers. Some are genuinely pleased with their publisher's performance.

However, the agreement between author and publisher nearly always favors the publisher. The writer loses control over the destiny of the book once it is published. In many cases, the writer is often at the mercy of an editor who might see the work in a different light and who changes or edits the work as he or she sees fit.

If your book doesn't sell by itself through word-of-mouth, its chances of getting much advertising support from a large publisher are slight. A big publishing house has many hundreds of books to sell. It cannot and does not promote each one heavily. Such

4

publishers work on the premise that a few of the titles will sell enough copies to pay their entire overhead.

Understandably, then, when a publisher has a "name" author who brings out a new book every other year, it can afford to publish many lesser-known authors, since the "name" author is subsidizing the whole operation through his or her book sales.

On rare occasions, a book sells without much publicity or fanfare through word-of-mouth. If it does occur, it is usually **after** the publisher has made some effort to get the book into bookstores.

To give you an idea of the way in which your manuscript is treated and the criteria used to determine if it is worthy of publication, the following information should help.

What Really Happens To Your Manuscript When It Arrives at a Publishing House

Although individual publishers operate different from each other in some ways, the basics are the same. There is one person (or group of people) who is responsible for answering queries and reading manuscripts. In answer to queries, they will solicit those manuscripts which they feel have some promise. Though some of the larger publishing houses have recently adopted a policy where they will not even open an unsolicited manuscript due to various legal and time constraints, most of the smaller houses will review all incoming material. Unsolicited manuscripts, however, are thought of as being the mark of an amateur and are commonly referred to as "the slush pile" or "over-the-transom."

My former company, which I've sold, now is called the imprint, Enterprise • Dearborn. Unsolicited manuscripts are received each year with one to five percent that actually go to print. Out of that percentage, the books usually all sell with one per year going beyond expectations.

Unsolicited Manuscripts

The slush pile consists of just about everything that anyone has the nerve to put in the mail. Most of it is pretty bad. Professional, experienced writers query first or work through an agent. In my own publishing company, over-the-transoms have included handwritten poetry by teenagers, treatises on the nonexistence of God, manuscripts by elderly people who have finally finished their novels and numerous, dubious get-rich-quick schemes.

Somebody has to open these pieces of mail and take a look at them. They will even get read by an editor if at first glance they show a glimmer of promise. The editor in my previous company found one or two gems among the slush, but that is the exception rather than the rule. Usually these are things sent in by amateur writers who have only seen the name of the publishing company somewhere and who are unaware of the publisher's goals.

If you want to avoid a by-return-mail rejection or (worse yet) no reply at all, it is usually best to query. You won't be wasting a lot of time and postage or run the risk of having your manuscript lost, marred or destroyed.

The Editor's Role

If by sheer chance your manuscript happens to catch the eye of an editor responsible for the reading of manuscripts, there follow a few well-defined steps. Usually you will be sent a questionnaire which asks you to outline your experience and qualifications, list your other published works, provide some concrete suggestions for marketing your book and explain why your book is so radically different from others on the same subject that the publisher would be justified in risking thousands of dollars publishing and promoting it.

Your answers on this questionnaire provide answers to these questions, but they also show how well you can put your thoughts down on paper, how much experience you have had and to what extent you are willing to help sell your book. If you are not interested in doing some of the promoting, why should the publisher be interested in doing all the work?

If the editor is satisfied with your questionnaire and decides that you are at least semi-versed in the mechanics of publishing and promoting books, he or she will put together a sales package that must be presented to the publisher and the marketing staff.

This proposal includes a discussion of your book in synopsis form, its advantages and disadvantages, some informal financial estimates and some initial avenues for marketing it. If it looks good on paper and your editor is in a brave mood, a sales presentation will be made to the publisher, and usually to the production and marketing departments, in an attempt to convince them to accept your book for publication.

The Publisher's Role

If the publisher is pleased with the presentation and marketing feels they can sell enough copies to justify the initial investment, only then will it leave the editor's hands. The publisher and marketing staff will look over the manuscript and decide if further discussions are necessary.

The further discussions include formal financial considerations, which are broken down into author's advance, editing costs, typesetting costs, paper costs, size of the printed book, printing process involved, plate making, binding and cost-per-copy printing. A marketing proposal is then prepared, sometimes by the editor but most often by the marketing department. This outlines the areas in which your book could be promoted in the most economical manner. Also taken into consideration are the promotion costs which include the preparation of the actual materials (artwork, design, typesetting), printing, purchase of space, list rental, postage, sales force efforts and miscellaneous costs.

If you have been published before, the editor will probably call on the people who worked with you in the past to determine whether or not they found you cooperative and easy to work with. News travels fast. Editors travel fast as well; the publishing industry is notorious for job-hopping. If there was ever a major disagreement between you and a publisher, be aware. There are always two sides to a story. But a publisher simply can't be bothered with a person considered tough to work with. Everyone's job seems tougher, no matter how well you write.

Your references, along with the formalized production and marketing cost estimates, will then be presented to the publisher who makes the final "yes" or "no" decision. Many books make it to this point, only to be rejected because of high costs or less-than-glowing references. If your manuscript does make it past this point, however, you can expect the greatest thrill in many a writer's lifetime----the letter or phone call stating that they are interested in publishing your book.

Being contacted at this point means that the cost estimates turned in by the production and marketing departments came out favorably in comparison with the sales estimate. In other words, the publisher has reached the conclusion that your book can bring in enough sales revenue to justify each and all of the various expenses involved in producing, distributing and advertising the book.

It normally takes 5,000 to 10,000 book sales for the publisher to break even, as previously mentioned.

Acceptance or Rejection

Most writers never realize that their manuscripts are accepted or rejected on the basis of very precise criteria. Instead, many believe they are turned down on the mere whim of an editor. Usually the opposite is true. The editor is the person who is pulling for your book, and if you have hopes of seeing your book in print through a conventional publisher, you should make every effort to get (and remain) on the good side of the editor. At times, they are your only friends, and in most cases, they are like salespeople, trying to sell their publisher on your book.

A good editor knows almost instinctively what will sell to the publisher and what won't. They know what the publisher wants and what the publisher won't even consider for a moment. So if your manuscript arrives through the slush pile in a condition or format which is not absolutely professional, you are making the editor's job harder and lessening your chances of the manuscript being read. Professionalism counts in this business, and the more polished and sophisticated you appear through your manuscript, the more you will be taken seriously.

There are those inevitable occurrences, however, when even the best, most professional manuscript receives an instant rejection. Usually this happens when the subject is just not right for the publishing company or they have already produced a book on the subject. Sometimes editors will reject a manuscript without really knowing why, but there is something about it that turns them off. Sometimes they will send a short note in explanation of the rejection, but more often, time does not permit this. If your manuscript was rejected in this way, it would probably be a good idea to go over it carefully before submitting it to another publisher. Query next time. Don't send a complete manuscript until the publishing house asks for it.

Three other major requirements a publisher looks at when considering a manuscript are the following:

1. Author who understands the publishing process, including marketing and public relations, and is willing to participate in the process.
2. Expert in his or her own area.
3. Can get along with all members of the department.

The Contract

If your book is accepted and the company decides to publish it, you will be sent an Author's Agreement which will outline their responsibilities and yours. While a standard author's agreement does not exist, as every publisher in the country most likely uses a different one, there are several main points which will be covered.

What Is Included

The agreement will be dated and will contain your name (as author), your address, the publisher's name and address, and the tentative or "working" title of your manuscript. The agreement will call for the publisher to gain exclusive rights to publish and sell your book in just about any format (hardcover, paperback, audio tape, microfilm, microfiche, etc.). It will set forth the areas in which the book may be sold (generally, they include the entire world) and will mention a royalty amount which is paid to you in return for these rights. Most often the royalty percentage is based on the publisher's net sales. So if your book is going to be sold for $14.95 and you are offered a 5 percent or 10 percent royalty, it does not necessarily follow that you will receive $1.49 per book sold. The publisher must discount the retail price by up to 50 percent when selling to bookstores, retail establishments, wholesalers, etc.

Subsidiary Rights

The agreement may also grant the publisher the right to sell subsidiary rights to your book. Subsidiary rights include: motion picture rights, serial rights, book club rights, reprint rights, electronic rights, paperback reprint rights and foreign translation rights, etc. Generally it is any way in which the book can be sold or licensed in order to make money for both the original publisher and the author. Often the publisher and author split the money received from these subsidiary rights down the middle.

Time Length of the Agreement

The term of the agreement may be mentioned, although often it is "in perpetuity." This will outline the length of time the agreement remains in force and may continue until it is a matter your heirs will need to be concerned with.

Completion Dates

Completion dates will be spelled out in the agreement. Perhaps it will also state when you must have supplementary material such as illustrations in the publisher's hands and have secured copyright clearances for quotes included in your book.

The Advance

The amount of the advance against royalties will be mentioned in the agreement. For a brand-new author this can be $250 to $1,000. But some publishers do not give advances under any circumstances.

Sure, you've read about the million-dollar advances top-selling authors have received in the past. However, that is for the established, bestselling authors. If an advance is offered, it may be paid in full on signing of the agreement or may be paid in increments as finished work is received from the author.

Publication Date

Along with author completion dates, most agreements indicate the publisher's completion dates. These are the time frames within which they expect to officially publish your book. This prevents a publisher from contracting for a book, having the author fulfill all of his or her contractual obligations and then never getting around to publishing the book. Most reputable publishers today will include their own estimate of the publication date, or at least say that it will be published and offered for sale in no more than one year, or something similar. If they do not do this, agreements usually allow you to cancel the contract without having to refund their advance money.

Making Corrections

The author will almost always be given the chance to see *page proofs* or *galleys* of the book before the final production steps. This is in order to give the author final approval of the typeset manuscript and to correct any errors. However, changing anything else beyond what was included in the original manuscript is what is called *author's alterations*, and the publisher will charge you for making them. This is usually spelled out in the agreement.

Royalty Periods

The manner in which the publisher is going to pay your royalties to you will be indicated in the agreement. This is generally semi-annually. Typically, publishers pay five to ten percent royalty on net sales to unknown authors.

Disclaimers

Then, as do most contracts, the author's agreement will contain a few disclaimers and caveats to the effect that any infringement on others' rights from material contained in your book is your responsibility; rights will revert to you if the publisher goes bankrupt; the manner in which disputes arising from interpretation of the agreement will be settled; and space to include other, more specific provisions.

Risks and Rewards

These contractual points between authors and publishers are typical ones. The publisher takes all the financial risk. If the book is successful, the publisher will earn most of the profits. It usually takes a typical publishing house the complete sales of the first printing just to recover costs. The author's royalty is paid on each copy sold, whether or not the book is a financial success for the publisher. Of course, if the book becomes successful, the potential profits to the author are far less than if he or she self-published.

My final suggestions about conventional publishers are: Contact them if you are at all interested in seeing your book published by someone other than yourself. If you beat the odds and they are interested in your work, talk to other authors they have published. It's a good idea to check references. Then ask yourself how much control you are willing to give up. With those answers, you will be prepared to make the best judgment for your personal circumstances.

Vanity Publishers

Authors discouraged by the high odds against publication of their work by conventional publishers, or those who have faced repeated rejections, are frequently seduced by advertisements appearing in most magazines of interest to writers. They read something like this:

"MANUSCRIPTS WANTED!
Your Book Published in 90 Days!
FREE Appraisal!"

For a novice writer, that prospect has alarmingly magical qualities. Imagine, a publisher actually soliciting manuscripts! Unfortunately, these ads are run by vanity presses (or "subsidy publishers" as they prefer to be called) who too frequently promise more than they deliver.

What Really Happens to Your Manuscript in a Vanity Publishing House

The typical scenario sees the author packing off the manuscript to the address indicated in the advertisement. A few days later, the author receives a glowing "review" indicating that the book has great potential for success and that the publisher has agreed to accept it. This kind of ploy can turn the most sensible and sane person into an eager-beaver with cash-in-hand more readily than the promise of the Midas Touch. It is saddening to see the ways in which vanity presses prey upon the naive or inexperienced people in this country, especially those who have already been turned down by numerous publishers in the past. When a "publisher"—any publisher—tells the struggling writer that the manuscript has "great potential" and that they have agreed to accept it for publication, this kind of ego massage is hard to turn your back on.

So, with the writer's sense of euphoria working against him or her, the vanity press follows up with a contract which promises royalty payments to the author as high as 40 percent of sales, as long as he or she is willing to pay the cost of the first printing of the book.

Clues To Look For

That should be the first and second clue. No conventional publisher is going to offer a new author a 40 percent royalty. The customary royalty on books is more in the neighborhood of 5 percent, up to 15 percent. The second glaringly obvious clue is that no conventional publisher asks an author to pay production costs. That is part of the risk a conventional publisher takes, and precisely the reason why it is so difficult to be published through one. With the vanity press, you pay the cost of printing, and then you have to **buy** your books from them and share your royalties! This is after you have paid to have the books printed in the first place!

The real kicker in the vanity press contract is that it obliquely promises promotional efforts but does not outline the money to be expended, nor does it stipulate the nature and scope of their proposed efforts. This is another big clue.

Who Pays?

A vanity press doesn't need to sell a single book to make a profit. *You* have paid all production costs (and these are usually inflated), *you* will have to buy your books from them and the only books that will sell in any great quantity will be those *you* sell yourself. On top of all this, the vanity press gets a steep 60 percent commission on all the books *you* sell.

The vanity press makes all of its money on its mark-up over *printing costs* alone, and it is virtually uninterested in the aspects of publishing which affect sales of a book (these are: editing, advertising and promotion). They may promise that you will receive promotion in their contract, but my advice would be to have your attorney examine any contract before you get involved in a vanity operation. Often, the promises made are so illusive that when the time comes for you to demand satisfaction, you will find that you haven't a leg to stand on.

Editing represents a cost to the vanity publisher, but it is more of a hit-or-miss proposition than anything close to the professional assistance you receive from a conventional publisher's editors. Since the vanity press expects no potential return from sales, it gives only the slightest attention to this most important phase. Gross spelling and grammatical errors are corrected (this is called "copy editing") but little else. There are exceptions. Some people have reported that they met up with an especially zealous "editor" in a vanity press who wanted to rewrite every word.

What You Get for Your Money

Printing and binding charges generally run several thousand dollars with a vanity press----considerably more than a similar self-publishing effort would cost. Furthermore, frequent practice is to bind a few copies for the author while the bulk of the edition is neither bound nor even distributed. If you think of it, why should a vanity press print, bind and store 5,000 copies of a book they believe will never be sold? They certainly aren't losing any money. You have already paid all the production costs. If you look carefully, you may find that the contract stipulates printing, with binding entering the picture only from time to time, as the need arises. With no promotion and no advertising, that need is not very likely to arise. Ever.

Promotion

In terms of the promotional work promised, a vanity press usually provides review copies for reviewers, editors of other publishing companies for reprint rights consideration, and bookstores. Almost all experienced reviewers will throw a vanity press book in the trash the minute they see it. You can expect the same consideration from editors of other publishing companies. The reason is that vanity presses, no matter what they claim, will publish just about anything. The quality is usually poor, both in writing and editing, and the production shoddy. An important reviewer would not embarrass his or her publication by reviewing

15

a vanity press book. The first thought that crosses an editor's mind in a conventional publishing house is, "Why did the author succumb to a vanity press? Did dozens of other publishers reject it?"

Advertising

The advertising most vanity presses do is just enough to fulfill the oblique terms of the contract. The most popular technique is to "tombstone" many titles in a classified ad in *The New York Times*. Such an advertising method in and of itself is almost as inexpensive as it is ineffective. The only other advertising you are likely to receive is a description of your book included in their "catalog" with hundreds of other books. This catalog is sent to libraries and bookstores. Libraries and bookstores do not buy from vanity presses on a regular basis. Bookstores will seldom stock vanity press books since there is no demand for them. The one exception might be as a personal favor to a local author.

When To Use a Vanity Press

There *is* one benefit in working with vanity presses: They do get your book into print. If you simply want to see your book in print and are not particularly interested in what it costs, or in seeing your book sold after it is printed, then a vanity press might be for you.

But, as I've hopefully clarified, don't let the heady glow of apparent acceptance dull your judgment. Read the contract, and have your lawyer explain the fine points. Call the Better Business Bureau to see if there are any complaints.

Even if this description fits you, [a) you just want to see your book in print, b) you don't care how much it costs, and c) you don't care if people buy it], there is a cheaper way to do it. The following method is far superior to either conventional publishing or the vanity press options. Whatever your wants or needs.

And that method is, of course . . .

Self-Publishing

Do-it-yourself publishing is neither new, nor is it unique. But it is successful. Percy Bysshe Shelley, Walt Whitman, William Blake, Benjamin Franklin, Zane Grey, Gertrude Stein and----more recently----Robert Ringer and William Donahue, are all self-published authors. There are an estimated 750 authors today who have self-published successfully. And, as mentioned before, I've sold over 1.5 million books and over 1 million other information products using the methods I'm about to outline.

Famous Self-Publishers

Although everyone's motives might have been different, I'm willing to guess that many authors came to self-publishing for the same reason Mark Twain self-published *Huckleberry Finn*. He was unhappy with the relationship with his conventional publisher. Other authors, like Upton Sinclair, were unable to get their first books accepted by conventional publishers. Luckily for everyone who loves their work, these authors had the foresight and determination to self-publish their first works.

Still other authors, such as Zane Grey, the famous Western writer, came upon self-publishing through a totally unrelated but successful vocation. Grey was originally a dentist in Ohio. When the publishers to whom he submitted his work intimated that perhaps he ought to concentrate his energy on dentistry rather than literary pursuits, he brought out *Betty Zane* in 1904. Shortly thereafter, he gave up tooth repair altogether due to the success of his books.

Surely you will recognize names like Carl Sandburg, Ezra Pound, James Joyce, and D. H. Lawrence, but did you know that they, too, are all self-published authors? Conventional publishers felt that Joyce's *Ulysses* was too long, Lawrence's *Lady Chatterly's Lover* was too dirty, and Sandburg's and Pound's poetry would not be popular enough. Obviously, conventional publishers make some big mistakes.

Self-publishing is not uncommon. But is it difficult?

No. It does take work, just as much work as writing the book takes, and it takes persistence. But the average author can manage it.

You will not need equipment such as a printing press, nor will it be necessary to hire a staff of editorial pros and proofreaders or a battery of advertising agents and public relations people. Like the person who subcontracts the building of a house, you simply buy the time and effort from printers, editors and proofreaders as you need it. At the same time, you can do any and all of these jobs yourself. And often far better than you can buy these services on the open market.

A Big Benefit of Self-Publishing

Perhaps the most readily overlooked benefit of self-publishing is that you retain complete control over your work. You do not have to battle overzealous editors who want to change your words, nor do you have to spend valuable time convincing an editor that something you overlooked and want changed is important enough to have reset in type. When you deal with a conventional publisher, while not usually done, an editor can insist on changes which can in some cases adversely affect what you believe to be the quality or integrity of your work. And there isn't a thing you can do about it short of totally disowning the finished book.

Historically, authors have not received the most sensitive treatment from their publishers, as Mark Twain would certainly attest. There have been a few notable exceptions (Max Perkins's editorial genius is one), but it is my contention that the majority of authors today would rate their publishers' performance in this respect somewhat below par.

Self-publishing, where you are both the author and the publisher, is one sensible solution to this problem.

Why Selling Books and Other Information Products Is the Ideal Business

I started 18 companies before I got into publishing. The fields included confectionery, real estate, building design, franchising and cosmetics. I've also long studied business opportunities, searching for the perfect business.

Then I found it in publishing. In my opinion, the most ideal business in the world is selling information products. These include "paper and ink" products such as books, newsletters, Special Reports as well as tapes and videos.

Here are the main reasons why I believe selling information is ideal:

- Products are easy to "manufacture." You can get products produced in almost any city in America.
- There is a *high perceived* value for information. You have *substantial* markups. Profit margins can be high: from 10 to as high as 30 times cost is not uncommon. It's not the paper or the video tape people buy; it's the information.
- The trends all point to growing opportunities in the future in our "information age."
- You can live, and operate from, anywhere in the world. The business is completely portable and can be moved. This gives you an unsurpassed lifestyle.
- You have no *competition*. Your products are copyrighted. They are proprietary, cannot be copied and belong just to you alone.
- Your market is the entire planet.
- The business is not capital intensive. You can start with as little as $600.
- Business is not dependent on age, sex or nationality.
- You can operate with few or no employees.

- You have less government regulation in publishing than probably any other business, due mostly to freedom of the press----a constitutional guarantee.
- You are doing business with intelligent, high-quality people for the most part.
- You are providing a wonderful human service by educating others and thus making the world a better place. You will be proud to be a publisher.
- And when you sell the business, it's one of the most attractive and, therefore, very saleable businesses.

Chapter 2

Methods of Self-Publishing

Small-Budget Publishing

If you are on a small (or even a nonexistent) budget, you might consider contacting printers who might be persuaded to print your book in exchange for royalties to come. They absorb the printing costs and then receive 5 percent to 15 percent royalties on your sales. Though you will have to do some hard-sell talking, this arrangement is not unknown.

Another no-cost arrangement is based on finding a printer to manufacture the book and sell it. As the author, you receive payment in actual copies of the book. For example, 10 percent of a press run of 500 books will net you 50 books. These could be used to send to reviewers and selected promotional media members to drum up more sales. It would tend to have a pyramiding effect.

Co-op Self-Publishing

It has been said that, typically, writers share three distinct characteristics common to the profession: misery, obscurity and poverty. However, what one writer is unable to do alone, a group can sometimes manage quite well. An example of such a cooperative arrangement between two writers exists in the Magic Circle Press, a publishing house created by Adele Aldrige and a partner.

Each put up $1,000 to get their own poetry, prose and artwork into print. They published a work entitled *Not Poems*, which at last report is selling for $3.50 a copy. Magic Circle Press has printed 3,000 copies and has received $5,400 in income. Expenses for paper, printing and binding came to $2,951. Mailing envelopes were $59, promotion was $300 and postage came to $400. The net profit thus far has been $1,690 but includes much of their own free editorial labors.

Countless numbers of small cooperative presses are springing up around the country each day. Some are groups of people with common philosophical or political ideas. Small feminist presses are gaining rapidly, since these groups of women feel they have not been treated fairly within the publishing industry. Other groups have been instituted to service the small independent publishers. These groups promote, review and serve as fulfillment centers for small self-publishing operations. Advertising agencies have come into existence specifically to handle the accounts of limited-budget self-published authors. It is an industry which is continually growing. This is great to see happening. With the author dissatisfaction which is so common when dealing with conventional publishers, and the public's growing distrust of vanity presses, self-publishing seems to be the most sensible answer.

Not only does self-publishing benefit the author in innumerable ways; it is one of the easiest ways to get "into print." Although it will take some work to make your book a bestseller, the pursuit of that goal is probably one of the most satisfying endeavors on earth.

So, come with me and let me show you the world that can open up to you through self-publishing and how much pleasure you can derive from it in the process.

What Is Involved in Self-Publishing

There are some basic areas in which you will need to become familiar before you make the decision to self-publish your book. These areas include printing, marketing and advertising. Marketing and advertising, as you will soon see, are the most important tasks, by far.

Printing Options

Printing is a rather obvious requisite in any publishing venture. You must somehow get your information before the public in printed form. There are other areas of publishing which are not concerned with the actual printing of words (audio-visual publishing, for example), but as a book publisher, you will need to have your work printed on paper.

Saddle Stitch

The range of printing formats and styles varies widely among self-publishing authors. Some opt for simple photocopied sheets set on an electric typewriter which are merely stapled on the left-hand corner. This method works best on limited budgets when the information to be printed is less than about 20 pages. Of course, if this is the type of book or "Special Report" you have in mind, you may have it typeset, but many simply have it typed by an experienced typist. They then take the text to a quick-copy shop, have it reproduced and stapled in the spine. (See Figure 5.8 on page 102.) This method is called "saddle stitch" and is quite common.

Types of Binding

Other authors have too much information to fit comfortably in a saddle stitched format, so they go on to bound books. The binding of books also varies widely. There are paperback, hardback, perfect bound, library bound, Smyth sewn, side stitched and many different ways of gluing the pages together in the spine. A discussion of all these different formats will be presented later in this book.

The purpose of mentioning them here is to familiarize you with the "catch" words of the industry. When you go to your printer, he or she will be able to tell you what they have available and at what cost.

The Difference Between Marketing and Advertising

Marketing is an area often confused with advertising. While advertising is the actual offering of your product to the public, marketing most often involves distribution as well as advertising. You must get your books into the public's hands. There are two basic ways in which you can accomplish this. One is referred to as "direct marketing," and the other is working through middlemen, or, in this case, through distributors and bookstores.

Direct Marketing

Direct marketing is the practice of advertising your product so that the public may purchase it directly from you. This often takes the form of space advertising with coupons the customer completes and returns to you with payment, or direct mail in which you send prospective customers a letter and they respond with their payment and ordering information.

Direct marketing is the most cost-effective means of generating sales. This is perhaps the most inexpensive method of marketing since you must give distributors and bookstores a large discount. With the middlemen, you are indeed selling your books, but you must pay them through your discounts. It is my contention that direct marketing is more profitable for the self-published author.

Advertising is a subject which will be covered quite thoroughly later in this book. I'll show you how to prepare advertisements through which the public can order your book. If you skim through any magazine, it will give you a good indication of the many varied types of space advertisements. Some have coupons which you complete and return, while others list an address to which you write.

Direct Mail

Direct mail is another method of advertising. You probably receive direct mail almost every day in your home. This involves a letter telling you about the product and its benefits. The package will usually contain an order form and a business reply envelope in which you send back your order. Direct mail is a relatively inexpensive method of soliciting orders, but like anything else, it must be done properly. I'll lead you through the process.

The advantages of self-publishing are many and have been alluded to previously. You might ask yourself this: Why don't all authors self-publish their work? There are disadvantages, of course, just as there are disadvantages to most business ventures.

The Drawbacks to Self-Publishing

Probably the biggest drawback to self-publishing is the initial cost. You need money to self-publish, and there really isn't any way around that. You will probably need at least $2,000 to get the job done properly and allow you to advertise to the extent that you can realize a return on your investment. This figure is somewhat arbitrary, however, and depends on the length, size and binding of your book. Very short, typewritten, saddle-stitched books, Special Reports and pamphlets will cost much less. So will a short production run of a newsletter, computer disk, audio tape or video tape.

Minimizing the Risks

Self-publishing is a business venture that can be pyramided, however, so that your risk is very low. It is not like setting up a franchise operation in which you must invest several thousand dollars before you even begin to get started. It is more of a pay-as-you-go proposition; you alone are in control and make all the decisions.

Still, there are ways to raise investment money, which I'll show you. You won't need to risk your life savings as many people have believed in the past. In many cases, self-publishing need not be any more expensive than a really enjoyable vacation or your first year's tuition at college.

The most important thing to remember when considering the initial cost is that it is entirely possible you will net the return of your investment many times over. Self-publishing certainly involves less risk than most investments, and since it is your product and you are running the show, it would seem to me that it is far *less* of a risk than people take on the stock market every day.

Having Your Readers Finance Your Printing Costs

If you are really on a tight budget, there is a way to self-publish at very minimal risk of less than $600.

Before you print the book, you prepare a sales letter offering your book for sale at a "prepublication" special price. For example, at a $29 price for a $50 book. You mail the letter to 1,000 good prospects.

Your offer states you will ship the book at a date 60 days from the date of the letter.

Your cash received from orders can in this way finance your printing costs.

Of course, if you don't have enough orders to proceed, you can return the checks and not proceed. But be careful not to run afoul of any postal regulations.

Your "Business Sense"

One other disadvantage which I would be remiss in not mentioning: Some people simply do not have a "head" for business, no matter how talented they are in other areas. These are the people who can't tell a good price from a bad one, will not be able to deal with the outside help they will need and cannot keep records in any form.

If this describes you, I don't recommend self-publishing. Through the worksheets which follow, you will be able to determine if you do have the business sense to make a go of a self-publishing effort.

Let's take a look at the options again so that you may be better able to decide which path you really want to take.

Your Options in Publishing Questionnaire

Conventional Publisher	**True**	**False**
1. I am interested mainly in fame and fortune and the renown that being published by a major house would mean to me.		✓
2. I am willing to hand my manuscript over to an editor and publisher, and I trust their judgment in what they choose to do with it.		✓
3. I can accept the fact that I will receive only approximately a tenth of the total profits from the sale of my book.	✓	
4. Rejection is something that I can face easily, and I have the time and patience to send my manuscript to one publisher after another until one of them accepts it.		✓
5. I will be able to relinquish control of my work and will be delighted with whatever shape and form it is finally produced in and with whatever advertising efforts the publisher makes.		✓

Vanity Press	True	False

1. I'm not really interested in seeing any of my books sold; I want them only as souvenirs and gifts for my family and friends. _____

2. I have plenty of money to invest in the publishing of my book, and I can easily afford not to ever get any of it back. _____

3. I am very skilled in negotiating with people and can demand the quality I want from a vanity press, even if that means a lot of hard work and correspondence.  _____

4. I have the room to store bound books and flat sheets where they won't be damaged. _____

5. I have hundreds of friends and relatives who would buy my book just because I wrote it, no matter what the cost. _____ _____

Self-Publishing

1. I have a great desire to see my work in print and to have many people read and benefit by it. _____

2. I have the money available to invest in the printing and advertising of my book (or one authored by someone else). _____

3. I want to maintain complete control over my work and would not trust it to anyone. _____

	True	False
4. I have faith in what I've written, and I believe that thousands of people could use the information I offer and would buy my book.	✓	___
5. I would enjoy running my own small publishing company.	✓	___

What Your Answers Tell You

From the self-test above, you may think that a conventional publisher or vanity press may be more what you want than self-publishing. If you are interested only in seeing your book in print, any of the three options could be for you. Self-publishing is the cheapest method of the three.

If you are interested in conventional publishing, I suggest that you reread the introduction, which outlines your chances of having your book published and its becoming a success. Again, your chances are one in ten from the start, and ten to one against your book selling out of the first printing. Fame and fortune can come much easier through self-publishing.

If you don't handle rejection very well, I would advise against going with a conventional publisher. You will most likely be rejected by many publishers before one accepts your manuscript (if one ever does----remember the odds). Self-publishing can get you just as much approval as a conventional publisher, and you won't have to face a single rejection slip.

If you tend to believe that an editor somewhere knows more about your subject and can write better than you can, you can hire a freelance editor before you self-publish your book. On the other hand, who knows more about your subject than you do? If you are concerned about your writing abilities, it might be a good idea to have an objective acquaintance take a look at your manuscript before hiring a freelance professional.

29

If you have hundreds of friends and relatives who will buy your book when it is published through a vanity press, they will certainly buy it if you self-publish it. This way the total profit will go to you, not to the vanity press.

I'm sure you agree that self-publishing is a viable option to many authors. It is definitely something to consider. The rewards from the endeavor far outweigh the risks involved. You can certainly gain all the benefits normally associated with conventional publishers, and you can avoid many of the common disadvantages of vanity presses.

Now let's take a look at the steps involved in self-publishing your own book to give you a better understanding of exactly what is necessary.

Chapter 3

The Steps To Self-Publishing Your Own Book and Making It a Bestseller

Choosing a Subject

The very first step in self-publishing your own bestselling book is to select a subject with high sales potential. The book must have a mass market appeal if your goal is to exceed 10,000 copies in sales. By "mass market appeal" I mean that the average American on the street would be interested in buying and reading your book. While very few books fit this category completely, you can pretty well determine which books would come close and which ones wouldn't.

Let's take a few examples. Let's say you have an idea for a book about investing in real estate. Perhaps you are a realtor with many years of experience behind you, and you feel confident that you are qualified to write a book on the subject. What will your book need to say to appeal to the greatest number of people?

Widening the Scope of Your Book

One title might be: *How I Made a Million Dollars Investing in Real Estate in Dade County, Florida*. This book might be a tremendous success in a biographical format. But is the average American going to be interested in it? What about a 20-year-old woman living in New York City? Or a 45-year-old city bus driver in Tacoma, Washington? Probably, they will not be remotely interested. A better approach might be to widen the scope of the book somewhat. Through this, your new title might be *How To Make a Killing Through Real Estate Investing with Little or No Capital*.

See the difference? The average American is interested in books that will benefit him or her personally. Their interest is piqued when you tell them how *they* can do something easily and inexpensively. You must always consider your buying public in your choice of topics.

How To Form Your Own Corporation Without a Lawyer for under $75 has been successful largely because average people can do it all by themselves and can save big money in the process. If I had written my book with a format such as *How I Formed 18 Corporations by Myself for under $75*, it simply wouldn't have the same appeal.

On the real estate book, take your experiences and add some in-depth research. In this way you could show people from all over the country how to do what you did and not limit it to Dade County, Florida. If you didn't expand the locale, the only people who would buy your book would be those interested in investing in real estate in one small county out of the whole United States. You would be drastically limiting your sales market.

What Makes a Book Sell

A study by Doubleday and Company Publishers revealed it is the subject of a book, not the author's name or reviewer's comments, that is the key to a successful book. The subjects with the best sales potential in this country are money (earning it, investing it and making more of it----especially in today's economy), sex, health, psychological well-being, hobbies, numerous self-help topics and the growing seniors market. Although some fiction books seem to have been experiencing a shrinking audience in recent years, many editors are advising that the market for good, interesting novels will always exist, especially where the motion picture industry is concerned.

Unless you are not interested in large sales, which are necessary to make your book a success, it is probably best to avoid controversial or "protest" topics, or others with built-in audience limitation.

Watching for Trends

Some books that have been very successful would seem to be limited in market appeal. There are, for example, several bestsellers on the subjects of writing, gardening and other seemingly small-audience topics. Consider, however, the extent to which these two hobbies have burgeoned in recent years. More people are turning to writing as an enjoyable pastime, so more and more people are interested in buying writing books. Today, nearly everyone has a few house plants or a small garden plot, even those who live in apartments. So don't disregard a subject just because you don't know anyone who might be interested in it. Watch the trends. Certain things catch on almost overnight, and a good book on the subject is bound to become a success just as quickly.

As a publisher, I am constantly amazed at the number of people who have valuable information in their heads who have never thought of sharing it with the public through a book.

I believe there is at least one good book in everyone, based on the valuable knowledge gained from life's experiences. People are willing to pay handsomely for information that can help them in their daily lives and in areas where they cannot simply take a course or read a magazine article about it. If you have doubts about your subject's appeal, take a trip to the library, and ask the librarian to help you find information about the nation's pastimes and current interests.

Chances are that you will find hundreds of associations and clubs throughout the country which may be ideal candidates for the purchase of your book.

Preparing the Manuscript

Nearly every type of person in this country (including doctors, housewives, business people, auto mechanics, and hundreds of others) write books each year and have them published. Few of them are professional writers, or they would have jobs writing or editing, or they would be freelance writers and little else.

You do not need to be a professional writer to self-publish your own book, either. The information you have to offer to the public is what buyers are willing to pay for. But if you are not a skilled writer, how do you get that information to the public through a book authored by you?

How To Get Help in Writing Your Book

The most effective method is to place a classified ad in the local paper, writer's magazine or *Publishers Weekly*, for editorial help in preparing a book. Newspaper reporters, public relations people, advertising writers, librarians, editors with publishers and a host of others have skills which you can purchase on a part-time basis to help organize your thoughts and your material.

You might need help only to get a working outline together or the research material ready. A librarian is the natural choice to contact for help in researching your book, again on a part-time basis. Most people are happy to "moonlight" and make some extra money.

If the actual writing process is foreign to you and you don't quite have the knack for it, you can advertise for a "ghostwriter." These are professional writers who are willing to write your book for you from your notes and thoughts. They will provide you with the finished manuscript. Many writers are willing to do this, even though their names will never appear on the finished work, because it earns money for them and they are not involved in any of the publishing risks. As you may not be aware, a great number of the books on the market today were not actually written by the person whose name appears on the cover. Within the publishing industry this is common knowledge.

There are many reasons for using a ghostwriter and certainly nothing odd or unethical about it.

Whatever your reasons, here are some of the most commonly asked questions about ghostwriters.

"What is a ghostwriter?"

This is a professional writer who is willing to do the writing and have it appear under someone else's name. A ghostwriter is different from a collaborator because the latter is given credit as a coauthor. Most autobiographies list the credits something like this: "By Bethany Movie Star *with* John Collaborator," or "By Bethany Movie Star *as told to* John Collaborator." A ghostwriter receives no such recognition.

"How is a ghostwriter paid?"

Usually a flat rate, often on a per-page basis. For research (including library time, reading, background interviews, etc.), they are usually paid by the hour. Sometimes ghostwriters receive a flat fee when the project is handed over. Ghostwriters usually do not share in the royalties of the author, as do collaborators. But there are exceptions.

"Why would anyone want to be a ghostwriter?"

There are several reasons. The ghostwriter gets paid for doing the work whether or not the finished product is a success or even gets published. Second, many feel that they would rather be writing and getting paid for it than sitting idle. Third, some writers simply enjoy working with interesting, idea-oriented people. Ghostwriting allows them to become knowledgeable in new fields. Fourth, writers genuinely enjoy their craft. Ghostwriting allows them to become someone else, to "disappear" behind the author and speak in someone else's voice. They like the versatility of writing in many different styles----in effect "becoming" different people. The best ones can write a fictionalized autobiography for a female celebrity and immediately switch gears and write political speeches for a foreign diplomat. Some writers thrive on the variety.

"How do I find a competent ghostwriter?"

The first place to start would be *Literary Market Place*, published by R. R. Bowker Co. This annual publication can usually be found in most public libraries. Check under the classification of "Freelance Editorial Services." These are people who will edit, polish, rewrite, clarify, coauthor (collaborate) or ghostwrite material. Some are agencies operating a clearinghouse of available writers, and some are individuals. Contact them by mail or phone, and emphasize that you are interested in a ghostwriting arrangement. Some may not be willing to work under these conditions, but many will be happy to discuss it with you.

Another source would be *Publishers Weekly*, a weekly trade journal for publishing company staffs, also published by R. R. Bowker. Look in the classified section in the back of the magazine. You're likely to find leads in the "Positions Wanted" and "Agencies" sections.

Writer's Digest is another source to consult. This is a monthly magazine for and about writers and is peppered with ads for editorial services.

Using a more direct approach, you might consider placing advertisements for a ghostwriter much as you would place an ad for a new employee. A classified advertisement in *Writer's Digest* will probably bring you a mailbox full of replies from all over the country. If it is necessary for you to maintain close and convenient contact with your ghostwriter, consider an ad in your local news-paper. Replies will come from librarians, college students, home-makers, teachers and professors, local freelance writers, in addition to newspaper reporters and staff writers on local magazines. Choose the ones who have the most experience in your field.

"What makes a competent ghostwriter?"

As with any situation in which you will be working closely with another person, the personal relationship is important. Can you communicate with the prospective ghostwriter, and vice versa? Do you share a mutual trust and respect? Does the writer grasp your goals and aims quickly? Is the writer an agreeable person to work with? Are there any other obligations which will interfere with the work being done for you? Is the writer open to suggestions and willing to make whatever necessary revisions are needed before getting down to the final copy?

Of equal importance is the writer's talent and ability. Ask to see samples of his or her work. Does the writing style seem similar to what yours would be? Can the writer write and sound like you? In other words, if you are planning a simple "how-to" manual on a popular subject, try to locate a writer with a style that is concise and easy-to-understand. If your subject is technical in nature, locate a writer with a background in or familiarity with your topic.

The rate of pay the writer will accept is another important consideration. The best guideline would be: Pay what it's worth to you. Don't try to get the cheapest writer available; you may end up with a shoddy job. Be flexible. An experienced, professional writer will command a higher price. For general guidelines on rates, consult *Writer's Market*, published by *Writer's Digest* (available in most public libraries). There is a listing of the "going rates" for all types of writing. Generally, you should expect to pay at least $10 to $25 per page, or a flat rate of $500 to $2,000 for a book. But you can pay as much as $10,000 to $15,000 or more, depending on credentials. Sometimes a ghostwriter may request an advance, retainer or a percentage of royalties. This is up to you. I feel that a 50/50 split on royalties can be fair to both if there is little or no up-front fee.

"How would I write an ad for a ghostwriter?"
An example of an ad for a ghostwriter for an autobiography can be very short, something like this:

> "Writer needed to assist with autobiography. Send resume and writing samples to..."

If your needs are more specific, you might place an advertisement something like this:

> Ghostwriter wanted to work on a "how-to" start your own computer cleaning company book-length manuscript. Talent in writing and experience in the business field essential. Send resume and samples to ..."

When you get replies, read the sample carefully. Contact those who interest you, and arrange a meeting to discuss the project, the rate of pay, the style, length and time requirements.

Once you have agreed upon a rate and time frame, you will want to have your ghostwriter sign an agreement. Essentially, this is a contract whereby you detail the conditions of your working relationship and each other's obligations. Figure 3.1 is an example of a useful agreement.

Figure 3.1 Ghostwriter Agreement

GHOSTWRITER AGREEMENT

The date of this Agreement is: _____

This Agreement is made between ___(ghostwriter)___ , (hereinafter referred to as "Writer"), and (your name)___ , (hereinafter referred to as "Author" or "Publisher").

Author/Publisher hereby contracts with Writer to provide certain Work under Author's/Publisher's specifications. All Work that is generated under this Agreement, including copyright shall be a "work for hire" or become the sole property of the Author/Publisher. Writer hereby agrees that he or she will keep the nature of his or her written assignments and the fact that Work will be published under the name of the Author/Publisher strictly confidential.

Author/Publisher agrees to pay Writer $_____ per page for a final draft of Work. Research, typing, copying or other miscellaneous expenses in producing this Work shall be borne by the Writer. Acceptability of written Work, including specifications and form thereof, shall be at the sole discretion of Author/Publisher. Work may be stopped at any time at the sole discretion of Author/Publisher.

Writer fully understands that aforementioned fee is full and complete for any Work covered under this Agreement, and that no further compensation or royalties will be paid should any of the Work be published at the discretion of the Author/Publisher.

Writer agrees to take full responsibility and indemnify Author/Publisher for costs of any copyright infringement action including damages and attorney's fees which occur as a result of the Work.

Writer acknowledges that all confidential ideas for Work covered under this Agreement have been supplied by Author/Publisher and are exclusive property of Author/Publisher. Writer further acknowledges access to certain of the Author's/Publisher's trade secrets. Writer agrees not to produce any Work similar to or competitive with the Work covered under this Agreement at any time or otherwise compete with Author/Publisher, directly or indirectly.

This Agreement is for a period of _____ days and is cancelable by either party upon written notice. It shall automatically renew for additional and consecutive 30-day intervals unless terminated by either party.

Signed:

Author/Publisher: _____ Date: _____

Writer: _____ Witness: _____

Once you have the signed agreement, you can present your material in more detail to your ghostwriter. Prepare a table of contents and a synopsis. Have ghostwriter prepare a rough draft of the first chapter. Then carefully go over it, and make your suggestions and revisions. If satisfied with the ghostwriter at this point, have him or her proceed with your work. If not, it's better not to go any further with the project.

Typing the Manuscript

Once the manuscript is ready to be taken to the printer for quotes or for typesetting, you can hire a typist to prepare the final manuscript. If it is typed without errors on a computer disk or on an IBM Correcting Selectric typewriter using a carbon film ribbon, your manuscript can then be put on your printer's computer typesetting equipment or photocopied. This will save you hundreds (or even thousands) of dollars in typesetting and printing costs. Before you prepare the final manuscript, discuss the specifics with a printer. In any case, whether you have your book on a disk, photocopied or typeset, the manuscript should be in perfect form, entirely free of errors and exactly as you want it.

You will receive galleys or page proofs. If you make corrections on these proofs that are different from what was on the manuscript, you will be charged for alterations. Obviously, it's best to have everything exactly as you want it to appear in print before it goes to the typesetter.

Desktop Publishing

As quickly as this new, revised edition of this book is printed, computer technology will also have changed. Print cannot seem to keep up with the speed of the ever-changing world of computers.

Desktop publishing is turning into a household word. But what is it?

Desktop publishing refers to the capability of a person not trained in graphic design to be able to create professional, effective graphic images at home or in the office without hiring professionals. People who have little or no graphic design background but wish to publish their own book, magazine or newsletter can now create attractive, effective printed material.

You might say that you don't have one artistic bone in your body and that a computer will not cure that problem. But through your experiences of reading and analyzing printed material, you have gained skills in design.

If you simply want to write technical literature and wonder why graphic design is important to publishing your book, think carefully about the books or manuscripts that have caught your eye. You'll have to admit that appearance as well as content is very important in written communication.

Effective graphic design is the difference that will cause a consumer to choose one book on the same subject over another. Consumers do judge a book by its cover. The book must look as appealing as possible.

Appearance also applies to the readability of a book. Readers don't want to struggle reading print or poorly designed graphics. Effective graphics help your readers make a decision to purchase a particular publication based on their emotional and intuitive feelings about your product.

This book will not train you to use your desktop publishing hardware and software. Tutorials and training manuals for whatever type of system you have will guide you with the basic commands.

Regardless of whether you use an IBM PC/AT, an Apple Macintosh, Ventura, Aldus PageMaker or any other system available, all the combinations are capable of producing the concepts that your creativity can invent.

Desktop publishing has saved even large corporations a lot of money and time by saving steps in going right from disk to film.

The film then is used to make the printing plates to go to print. The following steps show the difference between the conventional method and the desktop publishing method. Steps 1–6 can be done in-house. The savings come from time and not having to prepare high resolution (typeset) output that the film is made from.

CONVENTIONAL		DESKTOP	
1.	Typeset Manuscript	1.	Enter Manuscript
2.	Typeset	2.	Output Galleys
3.	Output Galleys	3.	Proofread
4.	Proofread	4.	Enter Corrections
5.	Typeset Corrections	5.	Output Corrected Galleys
6.	Output Galleys	6.	Reproof
7.	Reproof	7.	If OK, Disk to Film
8.	If OK, Output Type	8.	Printing Plates
9.	Final Proof	9.	Print
10.	Film		
11.	Printing Plates		
12.	Print		

Both experienced and beginning publishers can increase efficiency and profitability by learning desktop publishing skills. By experimenting with the creative processes of desktop publishing, you will continue to improve your work and save yourself a lot of money. (See pages 77–83 for more complete information.)

Avoiding Rewrite

Writers are notorious for wanting to change practically everything once they see their work set in type. Maybe that's why conventional publishers will charge the author if alterations on the galleys or page proofs are made. This serves as a deterrent to rewriting the whole manuscript. You must give yourself a cut-off limit after which you will consciously try to leave things as you have written them. If not, you can spend your lifetime rewriting and never get your book into print.

Retain your original manuscript in all cases, and store it in a fireproof box or bank safe deposit box. I won't go so far as to say that publishers are careless, but they are human, just like the mail carrier. As long as you provide a legible, duplicate copy, there is no reason to submit an original to a publisher or to a printer because it can be lost.

Writing for the Reader

A book about creating a bestseller wouldn't be complete without some information about putting words and sentences together to form a readable unit. Although there is no quick, magical formula as far as I know, I have found that the best route is always simple, clear writing, easy to understand by someone with an average education. The newspaper industry reports that to make your writing readable to the majority of Americans, you should write on a sixth grade level. In other words, a student in the sixth grade doing reasonably well should be able to read what you write, understand most of it and be able to tell you what it means.

Other Tips

1. Avoid the temptation to use a long word when a short one will do just as well. If you simply can't use a short word, include a glossary in your book, or explain the meaning in the text. This occurs most commonly in technical writing or in an area in which occupational jargon is frequently used.
2. The purpose of writing is to communicate something you know. It is not necessary to impress. The exceptions to this rule may be scholarly writing or educational writing for peers, or fiction and poetry. The effect of obscurity in these areas is often considered a skill.

3. Use simple, declarative sentences. Vary their length and position enough to make your writing interesting rather than monotonous.

4. Before you begin to write, read several pages of work you admire from another writer. Don't consciously try to copy his or her style, of course, but get into the mood for writing. Chances are good that if you enjoy a particular writer's style, your readers will too.

5. Use the precise word to express exactly the meaning you are trying to convey. If you don't know the dictionary definition of a particular word, look it up before using it.

6. Try to write as you speak. This makes writing more interesting. But if you tend to ramble when you talk, don't use a tape recorder and transcribe from it. You may speak ungrammatically while your writing is better.

7. Avoid colloquial or slang words and phrases. Most of these types of things come and go in style and usage. Readers several years down the road won't know what you're talking about. Also, slang can change meaning fairly rapidly.

8. Use action words which tend to conjure a mental picture for the reader. Put sight, smell and taste into your writing.

9. Try to be straightforward and precise. Avoid phrases such as "very big." How big? Compared to a pinhead or an elephant?

10. Vary paragraph length, but aim for short paragraphs in the main. Tests have shown that readers are more apt to read short paragraphs over long ones. If your subject absolutely needs a lengthy paragraph, see if you can reword it so that it can be separated into two.

11. Put the words you want to emphasize in the beginning of the sentence. Put the sentence you want to emphasize at the beginning of the paragraph. Put the paragraph you want to emphasize at the beginning of the chapter.

12. After you've written a chapter or several pages, put them aside for at least an hour so that you can approach it with a fresh mind. Revise and edit as many times as it takes until it feels right. Cut words that do not add to your message. Your writing can always be improved, but avoid the tendency to be verbose.

13. Be yourself. Even if you're writing textbooks, a little personal insight or something that will show the reader that you are a human being underneath it all will add interest. Readers want to believe in you, they want to follow your advice and they want to get to know you. If you allow your personality to show through the written word, you have made their reading much more pleasurable.

14. Have a dictionary and thesaurus handy at all times. You might also consider having a handy spelling dictionary, a spell check software program, a dictionary of quotations and a quick reference of synonyms and antonyms available. A grammatical guidebook is also recommended. The University of Chicago's *The Chicago Manual of Style* is a standard.

Writing is one of the most difficult tasks. It provides a stimulating mental workout for anyone attempting it. But it is also one of the most productive things you can do. You are creating an original work as you write, and in the case of fiction you are actually making up a new and separate reality complete with human beings. It's truly a remarkable feat.

Getting Professional Help

So be careful when you write. Nothing is more aggravating to a reader than to have to continually correct your grammar or your spelling while trying to figure out what you're trying to say. If you just don't have a good command of the English language, and you don't speak correctly by second nature, perhaps it would be to your advantage to hire an editor or ghostwriter.

If this describes you, it is still very possible to write an excellent book full of valuable information which will benefit many people. You will probably find the job much easier though if someone else actually puts the sentences and paragraphs together for you.

Collaborations and Coauthors

Another low-cost method (if you still feel awkward while trying to write) is to collaborate with a professional writer. This person would do the actual writing while you provide all of the information. In your self-publishing venture, the writer could be an equal partner, sharing both the risks and rewards. Obviously, if a writer's name is going to appear on your book as a coauthor, greater pains will be taken with the writing of the manuscript. He or she will be infinitely more interested in the potential profit from book sales.

If you decide to do it all yourself, here are a few more tips on writing effectively for a general audience—

What Makes for "Good Writing"

Good writing is usually considered to be that which gets the message across to the reader in a manner readily understood. It also affects the reader in some way. It has been said that a good novel is only a "good novel" when it somehow changes the life of the reader. It must move people emotionally, must provide them with illumination into themselves or people around them, must make them cry or laugh, must affect them in such a way that they might see life differently. They must remember it, too. Nothing is more boring than a flat, emotionless, uninteresting piece of writing that says nothing and goes nowhere.

Researching Your Subject

Research is another area of great importance. You will need to become absolutely familiar with all the "ins and outs" of your subject if for no other reason than to maintain credibility. You cannot overlook a single area, and you must cover every contingency and possible question in your reader's mind. Before drawing up an outline, list all of the possible questions a reader might have about your topic from his or her point of view. Put yourself in the reader's place. Imagine you are standing in a bookstore looking for a book on the subject. What would your questions be? What would you want covered in the book? Most important, what would make you buy a particular book over a similar one on the same subject?

Once you have these questions, head for the library and do some work. This involves reading everything you can get your hands on that even mentions your topic. This gives you a realistic idea of what has been covered and what hasn't.

Mentioning Your Sources

Research also involves establishing a "Suggested Readings" list for your book and a bibliography. Even if you do not quote directly or paraphrase someone else, list the sources from which you gained valuable knowledge about the subject. Unless you have performed some totally new research under laboratory or scientific method testing conditions, you have garnered information from other sources besides your own imagination.

Even if you are a recognized authority on a subject, you will still want to quote directly or paraphrase another author, simply to offer some back-up for your statements. Particularly if your work is basically new information (or is controversial in nature), you will want to mention other people's contributions to the field.

By researching your subject you are gaining the knowledge which will effectively make you an "expert." You will also see how the subject has been treated previously, what was left out and what new advances have been made recently. You can then make sure your book is the best in the field.

Perhaps you might want to do some research which cannot be found in bound books or periodicals. Your subject may be such that it is necessary to interview authorities in the field, and you feel your book would be greatly enhanced by an original quote or two. How do you go about this?

Using Your Local College or University

Usually, your local college is a great source of information. If you have a question, most librarians will be happy to help you if you explain that you are writing a book and need some information which is not generally available. The librarian may be able to direct you to a professor knowledgeable in the subject whom you can interview and quote. Don't forget about local business people who can be knowledgeable interview subjects as well.

Interviewing Other Authorities

For instance, if you are writing a book about natural foods, you might interview a nutritionist at your local college or university. But at the same time, don't forget the proprietor of your local health food store. Since business people's livelihoods depend on their knowledge of their products, they can be helpful in providing accurate and up-to-date information. They can also guide you to the most recent and well-received books on the subject. Local tradespeople and proprietors can often be your best source of information. Also, college professors are often involved in their own writing and research and may not have the time to help you with yours.

Interviewing Techniques

When you interview someone, there are some basic steps to follow:

1. Come to the interview prepared with a list of questions. Never go in "blind" and expect the person you are interviewing to carry the ball. They want to know what you are interested in and can't be bothered with leading the interview.

2. Formulate your questions so that they cannot be answered with straight "yes" or "no" responses. Ask leading questions so that the person being interviewed must explain or qualify his or her answers.

3. Try to put the person being interviewed at ease. Be friendly and interested in what he or she is telling you. Don't come on like a hardboiled newspaper reporter or try to intimidate them with your manner.

4. Don't take up much of their time. Be prompt for your appointment, and don't hang on beyond about half an hour to 45 minutes. Most people tire of talking after that amount of time. If you still need more information, call back and make another appointment. You might simply ask your questions over the phone.

5. Never put a person on the spot. If they don't want to be quoted, don't press them. Personal privacy is one of our fast-vanishing human rights; don't be one to help it on its way.

6. Be aware of the value of a person's time. Write them a note in thanks of their consideration. Always end on a good note by offering to send a copy of the book when it is published.

7. If you intend to quote the person, get written permission. This can be in the form of an informal letter which states the exact quotation. It is simply signed at the bottom and returned to you for your files. Most people will go along with this.

8. Keep your facts straight. If they have said one thing, don't embellish it or put words into their mouths by making them appear to have said what you wanted to hear. Don't quote out of context, and never quote a person and then disagree.

For example, don't say, "John Doe of Doe's Health Food Store said . . ., but I think he's wrong and I say . . . ." That's playing dirty. If you don't agree with someone you've interviewed, don't quote.

9. Try to be relaxed and open during your interview. Be genuinely interested in what the person has to tell you, or don't interview at all.

Developing Your Idea

Another sign of good writing is a sound, well-thought-out idea. It must be a deep enough subject to warrant a book. Avoid subjects that can be covered just as well in a magazine article. No matter how much extraneous information you add, readers will be able to tell that you are just filling up pages.

One example of this might be the idea for a book on the personalities of cats. Let's say that you have always had cats as pets, that you've noticed how they all seem to have distinct and separate personalities, and that you'd like to write a book on your experiences with your cats. It could be approached in several ways.

First, you could write an article for a magazine in a humorous vein, recalling the many different cats you've owned, their names, how you chose their names, what they were like and how they were different from each other. That would be a good magazine article, but it would be tough to write a whole book about it.

To expand this idea into a book, you would need to research the history of cats and their relationships to humans, speak with several veterinarians about their findings and personal experiences, talk with other cat owners to see if they have had similar experiences and if they believe in your original idea. To take it beyond that point, you might speak with animal trainers and ask them for specific tips on training cats, where you might be able to offer your readers some guidelines for choosing a particular breed of cat, how to train it, how to avoid the cat's development of bad habits and how to treat "meaty" enough for a full-length book. Your own experiences peppered throughout would make the book, and you, come alive through the words.

Getting Ideas for Books

Other ideas for books seem to be around us every day. For fiction, most writers use their powers of observation. One thing these authors have in common is that they tend to have an uncanny sense of seeing through people----the ability to determine what they are really thinking and feeling. After all, if you are going to write and create people in your writing, you must know all kinds of people almost inside and out. An author I know can sit on a bus (and frequently takes the bus for this very reason) and overhear a simple conversation between two fellow passengers. He will write notes at the end of the bus ride to catalog the conversation somewhere in his brain for retrieval when a particular situation in a story or novel calls for it.

The Observation Technique

For instance, if you are sitting on a bus and two women are behind you discussing the price of meat, listen to what they are saying and, more important, what they are *not* saying. Perhaps one woman's husband was recently injured in an accident, and she has had to cut down sharply on the quality and amount of meat she buys. A writer will immediately sense a story line behind that snatch of conversation. The most interesting conversations are between strangers (frequently on a bus or subway) who are making polite conversation, revealing little bits about themselves. As an eavesdropper, you get to know them as they reveal personal aspects of their lives. To make a fully formed character, you merely fill in the blanks. Writers of "confessions" frequently use just such a technique, by imagining the woman's house, what her husband is like, what she might have been like when young, how they fell in love and how they came to be where they are now.

To fiction authors, no situation is ever dull. Even the most mundane and commonplace conversation can take on a quality where it can be the source of many good ideas. Some writers have even built entire books around everyday experiences where they have let their imaginations run wild.

Turning Gripes into Books

A valuable source of ideas for self-help or "how-to" books is listening to people's complaints and gripes. I came to write this book by listening to many authors who said, "I wish there was a common-sense guide to explain the steps necessary for publishing my own book. The publishing industry is so secretive. I would really appreciate a book that showed me how to do it in simple, well-defined steps." So, after I learned how to do it, I wrote this book for people like you and me who want and need this information.

The art of listening is one of your most valuable skills as a writer. Listen to everyone and everything. Try to understand what people are *really* saying, what they feel and what they think about. The sources of ideas for books surround us every day. If you don't believe me, take the bus to work for a week!

For further information on writing styles and ways of getting ideas, I suggest the books listed in the "Recommended Readings" section. These books have been of great value to me.

Choosing and Testing the Title

I can't emphasize enough the importance of the book title. Perhaps the most frequently disregarded element in conventional publishing is selection of titles. An author might spend years agonizing over the manuscript, only to sit down over a cup of coffee with the editor to decide on a title.

More than anything else, the title is what gets people interested in your book. The title tells potential buyers what your book is about in nonfiction books, so it must be appropriate.

As mentioned, one of the best ways to sell self-published books is through direct mail and space ads. It is a method of exposing your work to the widest possible audience for the fewest initial dollars invested in promotion. The title is of primary importance, especially to those who cannot examine the book before buying it. If you were selling the book through bookstores, which you may do later, the jacket also becomes important. But even a professionally prepared dust jacket can be of little use if it carries an uninteresting title.

Earlier some discussion was made of titles as they relate to book subjects. To illustrate the importance of a book title, let's use the book on cats that was mentioned previously. The book contains the information outlined earlier, but we are going to use two different titles. Which one do you think would sell more copies?

**"A Scientific Investigation of
Feline Personality
from an Historical Perspective"**

or,

**"How To Get Lots of Love
from Your Cat"**

The second example is a more humorous, personal approach. The first one sounds like it ought to be a textbook in veterinary school. Also, the second tells you what the book is about. It grabs your interest (if you are interested in cats, of course) and gives you an idea of the information presented. It also hints at the style of the book. As another example, would you have *this* book if it had been entitled *An Examination of the Publishing Business*? Maybe, but I don't think it's likely.

Title-Testing Techniques

Since a title is of such importance in publishing and especially in mail-order marketing, I have developed a technique of title testing that costs very little but provides solid market research data both for title selection and further advertising.

Let's say you've written a book on organic gardening, a subject of widespread interest today. How do you choose a title? One "how-to" approach is: *How To Grow a More Productive, Pesticide-Free Garden* or *Secrets of Organic Gardening on a Shoestring*.

To test the pulling power of these titles, run ads for both of them. You need do nothing more than place a classified advertisement in one or more gardening magazines. If you choose a publication which specializes in one facet of gardening, it will probably have a lower circulation figure (number of subscribers and newsstand sales) than one dealing with the entire gardening gamut. Advertising rates will be correspondingly lower in the smaller circulation magazine. There will be more information presented about choosing and analyzing your advertising media in a later chapter.

What should your advertisement say? It ought to read something like this: "New book being completed by professional gardener----*How To Grow a More Productive, Pesticide-Free Garden*. For free information, write . . .."

Developing the "Brochure"

What is the information? For about $25 per thousand you can have an 8½ x 11 inch circular printed in black and white containing the pertinent information about your book. It would include the titles you are testing so that you can use the same circular to respond to inquiries from all your ads. Vary the titles in the ads to test the pulling power of each.

The circular should also contain the table of contents of your book. This gives the potential buyer a very precise idea of what the book contains.

In addition, the respondent can be offered a financial inducement to purchase a copy of your book when it's hot off the press. Perhaps here you would say something along the lines of: "As a prepublication offer, I would be happy to autograph your copy of my book and give you a $2 discount from the advertised retail price. It will be off the press in 60 days!"

Finally, the circular should contain a coupon enabling a person to order easily. Allow plenty of room for the respondent to fill in his or her name and address legibly. Also stress that they will receive their money back promptly if for any reason they are not satisfied with the purchase.

You will find that some checks will begin to flow in before your book is even printed. And at this point you can begin to analyze several things:

1. *The title that brings in the greatest number of inquiries will always dramatically out-pull the others.*
2. *Your "conversion rate." This is the number of people who write for free information and then go on to purchase the book.*

It is also quite possible that you will receive enough advance orders to pay for the printing costs of your first edition.

At this point, of course, your book has not been printed, and you have not invested money in printing a book in which no one is interested or one that has an ineffective title. In addition, you have gained a good feel for the potential market acceptance of your book with an investment of as little as $100. If your title is effective and the book is priced right, you may receive many times that amount in checks from people who take advantage of your prepublication offer. You can then choose the most popular title and have your book printed.

This technique may sound odd to you, but it is rapidly becoming a standard practice in many publishing houses. To minimize the risk, a publisher will have an artist prepare "dummys" of several different dust jackets for the same book. These are tested in the manner described above. Whichever title pulls best becomes the final one.

If none of the titles or jackets pulls any significant amount of inquiries or orders, usually the whole book project is dropped. The reasoning is relatively simple. If no one is interested in buying a book or product of any kind, why produce it? It's far better to return the few orders and payments received if it's a loser.

Chapter 4

Prepublication Activities

At this point, as you are preparing your book for printing, you can lay the groundwork for promotion. An early technical point you can proceed with is obtaining the copyright.

Obtaining a Copyright

Copyrighting your book protects it from being reproduced in any form without your written permission. The importance of this protection is often overlooked by self-published authors. It could very well cause you a big headache if this step is not carefully performed.

The book need not be published to file for copyright protection. You may have the manuscript copyrighted using the same form you would use to copyright the bound book. When setting up the final drafts of your work, the title page or reverse of it must contain the copyright registration. The notice must include three elements.

1. The name of the copyright owner (you)
2. The year of publication
3. The word "copyright" and/or the symbol: ©

Copyright 1993 by Jane Doe or **© 1993 by Jane Doe**

Write to the Register of Copyrights, Copyright Office, Library of Congress, Washington, DC 20559. Request Form TX.

You will receive a multi-page form containing questions such as: author, printer, their names and addresses, date of publication and similar information. The copyright office will send you complete instructions for completing the forms. When you have done so, sign them and return with two copies of your book (or manuscript) and the filing fee. Uncle Sam gives you a well-deserved break by allowing you to mail the books postage-free. Make your request to the postmaster.

You will get back one copy of the form bearing the official seal of the copyright office. It normally takes about eight weeks. Keep the official copyright form in a fireproof box with the original copy of your manuscript as evidence of registration.

Figure 4.1 is a specimen of the most current copyright application form. This will give you an idea of what it looks like and what information you will need to provide.

Figure 4.1 Application Form

FORM TX ☑

UNITED STATES COPYRIGHT OFFICE

REGISTRATION NUMBER

TX   TXU

EFFECTIVE DATE OF REGISTRATION

Month   Day   Year

DO NOT WRITE ABOVE THIS LINE. IF YOU NEED MORE SPACE, USE A SEPARATE CONTINUATION SHEET.

1

TITLE OF THIS WORK ▼

PREVIOUS OR ALTERNATIVE TITLES ▼

PUBLICATION AS A CONTRIBUTION If this work was published as a contribution to a periodical, serial, or collection, give information about the collective work in which the contribution appeared. Title of Collective Work ▼

If published in a periodical or serial give: Volume ▼   Number ▼   Issue Date ▼   On Pages ▼

2

a

NAME OF AUTHOR ▼   DATES OF BIRTH AND DEATH
Year Born ▼   Year Died ▼

Was this contribution to the work a "work made for hire"?
☐ Yes
☐ No

AUTHOR'S NATIONALITY OR DOMICILE
Name of Country
OR { Citizen of ▶
Domiciled in ▶

WAS THIS AUTHOR'S CONTRIBUTION TO THE WORK
Anonymous? ☐ Yes ☐ No
Pseudonymous? ☐ Yes ☐ No
If the answer to either of these questions is "Yes," see detailed instructions.

NOTE

Under the law, the "author" of a "work made for hire" is generally the employer, not the employee (see instructions). For any part of this work that was "made for hire" check "Yes" in the space provided, give the employer (or other person for whom the work was prepared) as "Author" of that part, and leave the space for dates of birth and death blank.

NATURE OF AUTHORSHIP Briefly describe nature of the material created by this author in which copyright is claimed. ▼

b

NAME OF AUTHOR ▼   DATES OF BIRTH AND DEATH
Year Born ▼   Year Died ▼

Was this contribution to the work a "work made for hire"?
☐ Yes
☐ No

AUTHOR'S NATIONALITY OR DOMICILE
Name of Country
OR { Citizen of ▶
Domiciled in ▶

WAS THIS AUTHOR'S CONTRIBUTION TO THE WORK
Anonymous? ☐ Yes ☐ No
Pseudonymous? ☐ Yes ☐ No
If the answer to either of these questions is "Yes," see detailed instructions.

NATURE OF AUTHORSHIP Briefly describe nature of the material created by this author in which copyright is claimed. ▼

c

NAME OF AUTHOR ▼   DATES OF BIRTH AND DEATH
Year Born ▼   Year Died ▼

Was this contribution to the work a "work made for hire"?
☐ Yes
☐ No

AUTHOR'S NATIONALITY OR DOMICILE
Name of Country
OR { Citizen of ▶
Domiciled in ▶

WAS THIS AUTHOR'S CONTRIBUTION TO THE WORK
Anonymous? ☐ Yes ☐ No
Pseudonymous? ☐ Yes ☐ No
If the answer to either of these questions is "Yes," see detailed instructions.

NATURE OF AUTHORSHIP Briefly describe nature of the material created by this author in which copyright is claimed. ▼

3

a

YEAR IN WHICH CREATION OF THIS WORK WAS COMPLETED This information must be given in all cases.
◀ Year

b

DATE AND NATION OF FIRST PUBLICATION OF THIS PARTICULAR WORK
Complete this information ONLY if this work has been published.
Month ▶   Day ▶   Year ▶   ◀ Nation

4

See instructions before completing this space.

COPYRIGHT CLAIMANT(S) Name and address must be given even if the claimant is the same as the author given in space 2.▼

TRANSFER If the claimant(s) named here in space 4 are different from the author(s) named in space 2, give a brief statement of how the claimant(s) obtained ownership of the copyright.▼

APPLICATION RECEIVED

ONE DEPOSIT RECEIVED

TWO DEPOSITS RECEIVED

REMITTANCE NUMBER AND DATE

DO NOT WRITE HERE
OFFICE USE ONLY

MORE ON BACK ▶ • Complete all applicable spaces (numbers 5-11) on the reverse side of this page.
• See detailed instructions. • Sign the form at line 10.

DO NOT WRITE HERE
Page 1 of _____ pages

Figure 4.1 Application Form (continued)

EXAMINED BY

FORM TX

CHECKED BY

☐ CORRESPONDENCE Yes

FOR COPYRIGHT OFFICE USE ONLY

DO NOT WRITE ABOVE THIS LINE. IF YOU NEED MORE SPACE, USE A SEPARATE CONTINUATION SHEET.

5

PREVIOUS REGISTRATION Has registration for this work, or for an earlier version of this work, already been made in the Copyright Office?

☐ Yes ☐ No If your answer is "Yes," why is another registration being sought? (Check appropriate box) ▼

a. ☐ This is the first published edition of a work previously registered in unpublished form.

b. ☐ This is the first application submitted by this author as copyright claimant.

c. ☐ This is a changed version of the work, as shown by space 6 on this application.

If your answer is "Yes," give: **Previous Registration Number ▼** **Year of Registration ▼**

6

DERIVATIVE WORK OR COMPILATION Complete both space 6a & 6b for a derivative work; complete only 6b for a compilation.

a. Preexisting Material Identify any preexisting work or works that this work is based on or incorporates. ▼

b. Material Added to This Work Give a brief, general statement of the material that has been added to this work and in which copyright is claimed. ▼

See instructions before completing this space

7

—space deleted—

8

REPRODUCTION FOR USE OF BLIND OR PHYSICALLY HANDICAPPED INDIVIDUALS A signature on this form at space 10, and a check in one of the boxes here in space 8, constitutes a non-exclusive grant of permission to the Library of Congress to reproduce and distribute solely for the blind and physically handicapped and under the conditions and limitations prescribed by the regulations of the Copyright Office: (1) copies of the work identified in space 1 of this application in Braille (or similar tactile symbols); or (2) phonorecords embodying a fixation of a reading of that work; or (3) both.

a ☐ Copies and Phonorecords b ☐ Copies Only c ☐ Phonorecords Only

See instructions

9

DEPOSIT ACCOUNT If the registration fee is to be charged to a Deposit Account established in the Copyright Office, give name and number of Account.

Name ▼ **Account Number ▼**

CORRESPONDENCE Give name and address to which correspondence about this application should be sent. Name/Address/Apt/City/State/Zip ▼

Area Code & Telephone Number ▶

Be sure to give your daytime phone ◀ number

10

CERTIFICATION* I, the undersigned, hereby certify that I am the

Check one ▶
☐ author
☐ other copyright claimant
☐ owner of exclusive right(s)
☐ authorized agent of

Name of author or other copyright claimant, or owner of exclusive right(s) ▲

of the work identified in this application and that the statements made by me in this application are correct to the best of my knowledge.

Typed or printed name and date ▼ If this application gives a date of publication in space 3, do not sign and submit it before that date.

date ▶

Handwritten signature (X) ▼

11

MAIL CERTIFICATE TO

Name ▼

Number/Street/Apartment Number ▼

City/State/ZIP ▼

Certificate will be mailed in window envelope

YOU MUST
- Complete all necessary spaces
- Sign your application in space 10

SEND ALL 3 ELEMENTS IN THE SAME PACKAGE
1. Application form
2. Nonrefundable $20 filing fee in check or money order payable to *Register of Copyrights*
3. Deposit material

MAIL TO
Register of Copyrights
Library of Congress
Washington, D.C. 20559

* 17 U.S.C. § 506(e) Any person who knowingly makes a false representation of a material fact in the application for copyright registration provided for by section 409, or in any written statement filed in connection with the application, shall be fined not more than $2,500.

January 1992—50,000

☆U.S. GOVERNMENT PRINTING OFFICE: 1992-312-432/40,015

The Biggest Shortcut To Publishing Successful Books or Other Information Products

Here is the best technique I've ever found to publishing success. Write a full-page ad or jacket copy that sells the product *before* you publish anything! This forces you to clearly think through all the benefits from the prospective buyer's point of view.

And there are many other powerful reasons to do this, including:

1. Your product will have a clearer focus.
2. You may change important elements in the product. For example, emphasize important sections.
3. The organization of the product can often be improved.
4. The key benefits the product offers can often be enhanced.
5. You can get prepublication publicity at little or no cost by having promotional copy ready.
6. You'll be better positioned to prepare a news release.
7. You can start selling the product on a prepublication basis and start receiving cash in advance of completion.
8. This effort can sometimes result in cancellation of the product. You could save a lot of money and heartache if the more prudent decision is to not publish.

The "no-go" decision can be even more valuable than the "go" decision if the facts convince you in this direction.

Obtaining Free Listings of Your Book's Title

Library of Congress Number

Your book can be listed without charge in the *National Union Catalog*, which is used by libraries around the world to buy books for their shelves. This simple matter of registration gives you exposure to thousands of potential buyers without any cost to you except postage.

To obtain this Library of Congress catalog number, write the Chief of the Card Division, Library of Congress, Navy Yard Annex, Building 159, Washington, DC 20541. Include the following information in legible form (preferably typed):

1. Author's name
2. Title
3. Edition (first, second, third, etc.)
4. Date of publication
5. Publisher's name and address
6. Printer's name and address
7. If your book is part of a series, indicate which segment will be copyrighted
8. Approximate number of pages
9. Type of binding (hardbound, paperback, etc.)

You must apply for this listing prior to the printing of your book since you will be assigned a number which is to be printed on the reverse side of the title page as follows:

Library of Congress catalog number 00-00000

Other Free Listings

You can also get your book listed free of charge in several indexes published by R. R. Bowker Company, 121 Chanlon Road, New Providence NJ 07974. These publications include *Books in Print*, *Forthcoming Books in Print*, *Paperback Books in Print* and *Publishers Weekly*. Libraries, bookstores, large discount houses and other stores use these lists as sources for purchases. In addition, other publishers monitor the forthcoming books through reviews in *Publishers Weekly*, other review periodicals and *Forthcoming Books in Print* for various subsidy rights.

Also write to R. R. Bowker for the forms necessary to obtain an International Standard Book Number (ISBN). Your book will then be listed in *Subject Guide to Forthcoming Books*, which is also used by buyers and other publishers as mentioned above. The ISBN should also be printed on the reverse side of the title page. Libraries and bookstores use this number for ordering, inventories and publisher identification.

You will also want to make sure that your book finds its way (after publication) to the H. W. Wilson Company, 950 University Avenue, Bronx, NY 10052, for free mention in the *Cumulative Book Listing*. This, too, is a catalog used by libraries and bookstores in purchasing.

A Word about Publishing and the Law

As a publisher, it would serve you well to know some of the thorny areas you can get into by putting words into print. These pointers are not intended to substitute for legal counsel, nor are they presented to alarm you. But they will give you some insight of the considerations you must make.

Broadly speaking, you should concern yourself with the rudiments of copyright laws, the rights of privacy, libel and illegal reproduction.

"Copyright" pertains to words and the form in which they are expressed. It does not extend to ideas. Common law copyright laws place ownership of a letter with the *sender*, not the recipient. Therefore, you will need to get permission from the sender of any letter you might want to use in the text of your book or in advertising.

On "the right of privacy," the law is not quite as clear. If people do not wish to have their names mentioned in connection with the advertising or promotion of a product (such as your book), they have that right. However, if a person is a part of a news event, even if a bystander at an accident, his or her picture and name can be used without permission. But, if you obtain a written release, you'll never go wrong.

"Libel" is the derogatory mention of a person in print. This can be accomplished through either words *or* pictures. Check reprinted material for possible libel since you can be charged even if you weren't the originator. Truth is a defense, but make sure your sources are not rumors or fourth-hand accounts. Generally, it is a good rule of thumb to avoid mentioning names or specific organizations altogether. Also, do not be derogatory about an individual or organization without being aware of serious risks in doing so.

As for "reproducing material that is illegal," remember to avoid promoting lotteries, securities, money, financial schemes, stamps or activities which could be deemed obscene or fraudulent. Of course, do not reproduce material from a copyrighted source without obtaining written permission first. Since your books will probably be sent through the mail, you will want to be particularly careful in the above-mentioned areas since a separate set of statutes applies for that purpose. Those laws do, however, cover basically the same general categories outlined above.

Public Relations for the Self-Publisher

Public relations is more or less a catch word for a whole variety of activities you can become involved in as a self-published author. The first and probably most important of these activities is the news release.

A news release is formally a typewritten sheet of information about your forthcoming book. Less formally, it is known as a quotable news story arranged in a way so that editors to whom you send it can print it as is or with minimal editing. It makes newspaper and magazine editors' jobs somewhat easier since you have provided all the information for them. They won't have to make a decision about whether or not you're worth a story. They won't have to send a reporter to interview you. They won't have to spend a lot of time editing a reporter's story. If your news release is well-written, is newsworthy, and it arrives at a time when they are in need of news of that nature, you have a good chance of having it published.

Write your news release as you would a news story. Cover the most important aspects in the first paragraph, then elaborate on them in descending order of importance. Make sure that "who, what, where, when, why and how" are in the first paragraph. Use quotes whenever possible. If you are going to say that your book is the most exciting thing to come down the pike in a hundred years, place it in such a way that the newspaper does not appear to be saying it, but you do.

This is an example of a bad beginning paragraph:

> "This is undoubtedly the most complete, comprehensive and thorough guide on the subject ever to be published."

Rather, you should say something like this:

> According to the author, Mr. John Doe, "I've spent two years writing the most thorough guide on the subject ever published."

That gives it authenticity. It's all right to quote yourself, but don't make it appear as if the newspaper is making the statement. Leave that to the book reviewers.

Make sure your news release is newsworthy. Keep adjectives to a minimum. But make it peppy, exciting and of such immediate importance that it will have to be printed at once. Always put a date on your release. The majority of editors will ignore an undated news release. Dating it will give it a timely quality, indicating that it is indeed "hot" news----the thing editors are always looking for.

It isn't necessary to get flashy about the format. It is imperative that you type it, double-spaced, and that it is well written (at least of the same quality as the publications for which it is intended).

Figure 4.2 shows a few examples of news releases.

Figure 4.2 Sample News Release

NEWS!
FOR IMMEDIATE RELEASE FROM: Your Publishing Co.
(date)

Negotiations have just been completed between Your Publishing Co. and John Doe for publication of his new book, *The Secrets of Home Repair*, which will be off-press in August of this year.

According to a spokesperson from Your Publishing Co., Mr. Doe's book is "the last word in do-it-yourself home repairs. He explains every aspect of this previously complicated area in terms every homeowner will understand. It is the most comprehensive, complete and easily understood guide available."

John Doe, who has run his own plumbing and heating service company for 20 years, spent 18 months preparing this book. He has finally offered the information to the public.

Asked if this information would reduce his business, Doe replied: "No. My book won't hurt my business. In fact, it will help it. I've always wanted to help people understand the basics of home repairs, and talking to informed customers makes my job easier."

National advertising and direct mail campaigns are planned, and Doe will be a guest on several radio talk shows in the area in the coming months. He has been a member of the Anytown community since he was born. His firm is the oldest subcontracting plumbing business in the city, and he has plans to retire soon. "I'm interested in giving people the kind of information I wish I'd had when I bought my first home. My book shows how to take care of the most minor repairs, all the way up to handling major emergencies and minimizing damage."

For more information, write Your Publishing Co., 308 Main Street, Anytown, NY 00000.

###

NEWS RELEASE
FOR IMMEDIATE RELEASE----(date)

LOCAL MAN HITS THE JACKPOT!

Jack Smith, a life-long resident of Anytown, has just completed negotiations with Your Publishing Co. to publish his book, *What It Means To Win a Million Dollars*, about his experiences before and after winning the state's Million Dollar Lottery. The book will be available next month.

According to a spokesperson for the publisher, Jack's book is "a warm and human portrayal of the joys and unexpected problems that crop up when someone actually wins a million dollars. Jack has done a fine job of telling us what it was like to be a millionaire overnight----what's good about it and what's bad."

Asked what he hopes to be accomplished through his personal account of the event, Jack said, "I want people to realize that winning the lottery is not the greatest thing in the world. At first, I was beside myself—almost numb. I spent a lot of money on things I'd always wanted for my family. Then it started to wear off, and I got my senses back. Today, I'm just Mr. Average----I've still got my job, and I go to work every day. But I told the whole experience from beginning to end and what it was like for me. People are always asking me about it, and that's how I got the idea for the book. Believe me, the whole thing isn't close to what you'd expect."

The book is being printed locally and may be ordered from Mr. Smith himself, at 000 Main Street, Anytown, NY 00000.

###

Another form of news release is more versatile and can be printed in large quantities to be used as an "information sheet" or announcement. Its usable life is much greater than the dated news release. This is somewhat less "newsy" and serves as an announcement of your book. You can use this in many different ways. Mainly, you can insert it in all of your correspondence, no matter what its nature. You can even enclose it in your bill payments! That may sound farfetched, but you never know when the mailroom clerk or someone's secretary might be interested in your subject and be a potential buyer.

Send your announcements to a list of carefully selected book reviewers. Obtain this list from a publication known as *Literary Market Place* (LMP), published by R. R. Bowker Co., 121 Chanlon Road, New Providence, NJ 07974. If your local library does not have a copy of this directory, you might consider buying one from the publisher. It lists book publishers, magazine and newspaper publishers, freelance editors, book reviewers, review syndicates, book clubs, printers and wholesalers. You can make up your mailing list from the reviewers and from the magazine and newspaper book review editors listed. Send them all a copy of your announcement.

If you type the names and addresses on gummed labels with a carbon copy between the sheets, you will have an automatic mailing list, ready to stick on the review copies of your books when they are ready to go. If you want to be more selective, weed out those reviewers who do not seem right for your book, and include only those magazines which cover the subject of your book.

Figure 4.3 is an example of a news release/announcement that was used recently to announce a book published by my own company.

Figure 4.3 Sample News Release/Announcement

FOR IMMEDIATE RELEASE   CONTACT:_____(name)_____

                                                   (phone number)

HOW TO INCORPORATE WITHOUT LEGAL ASSISTANCE AND FEES IS FOCUS OF NEW BOOK

According to *The Wall Street Journal*, over 70,000 new corporations are formed each month in North America. In a recessionary period, that number is expected to increase greatly as more and more individuals are seeking the stability and tax advantages of self-employment by forming their own businesses.

Thanks to recent tax changes, small business people are able to enjoy better tax rates as well as fringe benefits by incorporating. Yet many hesitate to do so, balking at the complex process and high legal fees often involved. According to business expert and entrepreneur Ted Nicholas, "Lawyer's fees for incorporating range from $300 to $3,000 or more. Yet a little-known fact is that in many states an individual can legally incorporate without the services of a lawyer."

Nicholas has devised a system of self-incorporating that allows entrepreneurs to avoid the legal fees and confusion of incorporation. The book detailing this system, *How To Form Your Own Corporation Without a Lawyer for under $75*, is now in its 20th anniversary edition, just released by Enterprise • Dearborn ($19.95). With over 900,000 copies in print, the bestseller has helped thousands learn how quick, easy and inexpensive the process can be.

In clear language, the book details the many benefits of incorporating, including:

- Tax-deductible automobiles and meals
- Medical insurance
- Limited personal liability
- Improved access to raising capital
- Advantages of estate planning techniques

By following simple instructions, readers will learn how to incorporate without a lawyer at minimal cost. A complete set of forms is provided, along with a Certificate of Incorporation, minutes, by-laws and more. Once incorporated, business owners will be able to benefit from the many tax- and money-saving ideas Nicholas presents.

How To Form Your Own Corporation Without a Lawyer for under $75 ($19.95), 150 pages, 8½ x 11, paperback, ISBN: 0-79310-419-X) is available at local bookstores or from Enterprise • Dearborn, 520 North Dearborn Street, Chicago, IL 60610-4354. Consumers can order the book by calling toll-free 800-322-8621. In Illinois call 312-836-4400 ext. 650.

Dearborn Publishing Group, Inc., under the Enterprise • Dearborn and Upstart imprints, has become one of the nation's premier publishers of small business information resources.

###

As you can see, you will be able to send this type of news release to every friend, acquaintance, business client or associate and distant cousin in your address book. If you want to send this type of announcement to reviewers only, you will need to change the last sentence to read: "To obtain a complimentary review copy, please reply . . . ."

More P. R. Techniques

There are several other public relations steps which you might take. One is to make your name known in your local area. Remember that an article written about you by a reporter and appearing in your local paper may be picked up by the wire services and printed in newspapers all over the country. This has happened many times. Local magazines, local "shoppers" publications and independent papers are always interested in interesting events surrounding area residents. If modesty prevents you from contacting writers and reporters yourself, ask a friend or noted business acquaintance to write or call in the suggestion that you might make an interesting story.

Make friends with the proprietors of all bookstores in your area.

Send them your news release, and then drop by or give the owner a call about a week later. You may not come away with a big order for your books, but the contact is invaluable. Perhaps the owner might be persuaded to carry copies of your book on consignment. He or she might possibly offer to host an autograph party for you. Whichever the case, the exposure is most important.

Offer to teach a course in writing or self-publishing . . .

. . . through your local high school or college's adult education department. You would be amazed at the number of people from all walks of life who have "always wanted to write" or "always wanted to see my name in print." Teaching courses can also be lucrative. Once you have established yourself as an expert and have some teaching experience, you can teach your own classes out of your own home or rent a conference room for this purpose. Naturally you will make more money on your own rather than being paid by the hour by the school.

Write articles . . .

. . . for local, regional and national magazines. Some freelance writers prefer writing articles over book manuscripts. You can sometimes get more done and earn about the same (or more) money for the same amount of work. In any case, having your byline appear *anywhere* is going to boost your public image.

Make yourself available to address groups of people.

Sometimes high schools will have "career days" in which they invite adults from many different professions to speak to students about their particular lines of work. You might not be paid for this, but again, it's all in the name of public relations. You never know when a contact will come in handy. Local civic groups are always looking for speakers. Contact the Rotary Club, Lions, Elks and other civic or fraternal groups. Don't forget to investigate local writers' clubs. You can often sell your books as a result of these talks.

Offer copies of your book as prizes.

Just about any special interest group (such as gardeners, motor-cycle enthusiasts, car clubs, poets and writers, model airplane hobbyists, etc.) has meetings and sells raffle tickets to raise money at one time or another. If your subject is pertinent, donate a copy or two as a prize.

Contact local reviewers.

There are scores of people, ranging from housewives to attorneys, who write book reviews for local papers as a hobby. It is probably better to contact these people yourself rather than going through the book review editor of the paper. Get the reviewer interested in your book, and it's almost guaranteed that you'll see a review in print.

At times, it may seem that you're not making enough money in public relations pursuits to justify your time and expense. But I can't emphasize enough that goodwill and having your name recognized are most important aims. Every effort you make is likely to pay off in the long run, sometimes by a huge multiple.

Chapter 5

Printing Your Book

Pricing and Other Factors Affecting Printing

A great many myths exist in the area of the publisher's pricing of books. It has been my experience that when you are selling valuable information, especially information which is new and cannot be found in book form anywhere else, a relatively high selling price is not nearly as frightening to potential buyers as the author might believe.

Publishers Weekly, a trade magazine for the book publishing industry, indicates that the average price for hardcover books in a recent year was $18.30. Quality paperbacks averaged $6.57. Many professional, how-to and idea books are selling for *much* higher prices----$50 to $99; and still higher prices are becoming more common. Writers tend to feel immoral about selling a book for $50 if it costs only $5 to print. This could be the one reason why writers are often poor and publishers are rich!

If you are having trouble deciding upon a fair market price for your book, don't consider the printing and production costs as a determining factor. You must also count the time and effort you have put into writing and researching your book, and the money you will need to spend to get it into the public's hands. Also consider the value of information to readers.

The concept that works most successfully in book sales is similar to the marketing practices used in cosmetics. A lipstick that sells for $1 costs only pennies to manufacture. However, a large portion of the difference between cost and retail price goes into advertising. So it is with a self-published book. Your selling price breakdown should be like this:

A book with a $20 retail price:

Advertising and promotion	$ 10
Cost of production (artwork, graphics and printing)	3
Operating overhead	2
Profit	5
	$ 20

If there is such a thing as a "standard" in the self-publishing field, it is probably based on the equation of setting the retail price at about two times the production cost. This standard has undoubtedly accounted for many a self-publishing failure because it is dangerously wrong! What it fails to take into account is the vital margin for advertising. For instance, if your book costs $5 to produce and you sell it for $10, where would you get the money for postage, overhead and advertising, not to mention turning even the slightest profit? I like to see 5 to 10 times printing costs or more. Remember, you are not selling pages; you are selling valuable information. This really is the underlying key to pricing.

Press run is a significant factor in setting price. Cost of production drops dramatically per copy as your press run increases. But for a first-run title, with untested marketability, you may want to keep the press run relatively small to avoid costly overstock.

One way to determine marketability is to advertise with a prepublication discounted price. Orders generated this way give some indication of interest in a book, especially when the market is limited to a relatively small special interest audience.

Cost Considerations

The size and styling of the book you produce directly affects the cost of producing it. The factors entering here are:

1. Size
2. Number of pages
3. Paper vs. hardcover binding
4. Paper stock
5. Quantity
6. Number and kinds of illustrations
7. Number of ink colors
   a. on cover
   b. inside

Let's take a closer look at each of these elements.

Size—Most books are printed in something close to 6 x 9 and 8½ x 11 inch sizes, largely because they are the most economical. Each page will carry about 400 words of 10-pitch type, which is standard pica typewriter size. Other sizes of books are 3½ x 6 inch, 4½ x 7 inch (paperback). I like the 8½ x 11 inch size since it is easy to read while helping to create a high perceived value.

Small formats are more restrictive. Often they do not fit very well on bookshelves, and they might be more expensive than the 6 x 9 inch size because of paper waste. Too large a size is expensive and cumbersome and offers no advantage other than in reproducing large illustrations. Most oversized books are of the "coffee table" genre and carry a small amount of printed information among the photographs. These books will not fit into a bookcase either.

Number of Pages—This is something that your printer can help you determine. Depending upon the length of your manuscript, the number of pages in your finished book can vary greatly.

Smaller type can be used to shorten the appearance (and number of pages) of your book while larger type will make your book longer. You can also adjust the number of words that fit on a page by changing margins. Wide margins will reduce the number of words, and narrow margins will increase the number. Remember that the number of pages will directly affect the production cost.

Paper or Hardcover Binding—Production costs for paperbacks are less costly than for hardcover books by a few dollars to $25 or $30 or even more per copy. They are also lighter, printed on thinner paper and cost less to mail. However, if you want to offer something that a reader will perceive as valuable and luxurious, consider the clothbound hardcover. Another thing to consider is that a large percentage of books purchased are to be used as gifts. People today often give paperback books as gifts. Remember that you can have both cloth and paperback editions of your book. You can usually get 250 hardcovers and 750 paperbacks in a 1,000-book run. An 80-pound dust jacket on colored stock will enhance the sales appeal and perceived value of your book.

Paper Stock—Generally, a 50- or 55-pound weight is best for paperbacks with covers printed on a heavier, glossy "kromekote" sheet. For hardbacks, a 60-pound or heavier stock is preferred, except in the case of voluminous works such as dictionaries.

Quantity—As with all manufacturing, you will get a price break on larger orders. Your print run will depend almost entirely on your realistic estimates of how many books you can sell, which we will discuss later.

Number and Kinds of Illustrations—These range from simple line drawings and schematics to full-color photographs. Discuss the price considerations of your illustrations with your printer. Sometimes a line drawing by a graphic artist can be clearer and more attractive than a photograph. Costs of acquiring reproduction rights may be more than the costs of reproducing illustrations.

Some other details as to type of binding, typefaces, leading between lines of type and line lengths can be discussed with your printer and will depend somewhat upon the printer's equipment and capabilities. Make sure that you get the best quality you can afford in all respects and a typeface proven to be easily read without eye strain or fatigue.

Caveat

What follows is general information about some basic typesetting methods. However, new developments in desktop publishing are occurring daily. Before you have anything typeset or printed, check with a reputable computer dealer as to how the latest state-of-the-art technology affects your project. Today's standards are Macintosh computers with 300 dot-per-inch or higher laser printers.

Desktop Publishing

Desktop computers and reasonably priced off-the-shelf software for applications that include word processing, typesetting, page design and makeup, and illustration, are a real boon to self-publishers. This technology permits writers and self-publishers to take manuscripts all the way to professional-looking typeset and designed pages. And that requires only a little more effort than generally is involved in merely preparing a manuscript.

A few cautions, however, are in order. Even though computers and programs that run them are relatively easy to learn today because instructional manuals, on-screen tutorials and "help" screens built into software are in simple language and logical sequence, several days to a few weeks (or even more) may be necessary to learn the basics of a computer's operating system. The same is true for the application of each software program you buy. Once you learn one program on a specific computer system, however, learning the second program by the same manufacturer (even though unrelated in application) normally will require considerably less time because you're familiar with how information is organized within that family of programs.

Hardware——This is the *equipment* you'll need, such as computers (we'll call them *platforms*), printers, and peripherals such as scanners, modems and external disk drives.

Platforms   Two dominate desktop publishing. One is IBM Personal Computer (and its clones). All these usually are referred to simply as PCs. The other is Apple Macintosh, most often referred to simply as the Mac. Most graphics-oriented publishing software initially was developed for the Macs, but PC-compatible versions now are on the market for nearly all of them. Most number-crunching and database programs, on the other hand, were initially developed for PCs, but today they have counterparts that run on the Mac. So basically which computer you use today is largely personal preference, or more likely, which system is available to you (if you're not setting up a new system). Software is increasingly available to allow both Mac and PC platforms to work interchangeably with each other. Your computer dealer can guide you in selecting both hardware (a computer and printer) and software (the programs to run them) to best suit your specific publishing needs.

Printers   With either a Mac or a PC, you will be able to generate on plain paper camera-ready pages that a commercial printer can work from. Typically, this will be done through a 300 dot-per-inch (dpi) or higher laser printer. However, these two types of computers (and many others) can drive other printers. Four general types are available.

Impact printers commonly are considered dot matrix and letter quality. Both are similar to typewriters in that they strike through an inked ribbon to leave an impression on the paper.

A *dot matrix printer* creates letters and images with tiny blunt pins that strike the ribbon. The output from these printers generally is not good enough to use as camera-ready art for a publication. A dot matrix printer, however, may be able to give you not only text but very rough renditions of graphics. Also, it often can create a wide variety of differences in type sizes through file commands.

A *letter-quality printer* creates impressions on paper that are indistinguishable from the quality produced by a typewriter because letters are created by a hammer striking an arm of a daisy wheel bearing at its tip one letter of the alphabet (or a numeral or symbol). Ordinarily, a letter-quality printer cannot be used to output graphics that may be stored in an electronic file. Also, only a small range of typefaces and sizes exist, and these can be implemented only by physically changing the printer's daisy wheel.

Laser printers are another category of printers. They create images by fusing toner to paper with heat (similar to the way a photocopy machine records images). These printers operate very quietly, as compared with impact printers, which make considerable noise when striking the paper.

A laser printer has resolution much finer than that produced by a dot matrix printer. It can output both type and graphics. And often the result is good enough quality to be used as camera-ready art for a publication. Even if better quality is desired (say 1,250 dpi resolution instead of 300 dpi) for camera-ready art, the lower resolution laser print becomes a very economical proof of what is in the computer file.

Digital photo imagesetters yield the highest quality type and graphics from desktop publishing files. These imagesetters (such as Linotronic 300 and Linotronic 600) output electronic files created on PCs and Macs by exposing photographic paper with laser light. This photographic paper then is developed and fixed or stabilized in chemical baths (normally in automatic processors that can be used in an office environment). Type from an imagesetter is very good quality----1,250 dpi or higher resolution. This is the type of printer used by many commercial typesetters. Service bureaus also usually output your files on imagesetters. Buying output from service bureaus at a few dollars per page often is more practical for most self-publishers than is investing many thousands of dollars in a photo imagesetter.

With a photo imagesetter, service bureaus can produce from your computer files black-on-white paper pages to be used as camera-ready art, plate-ready negatives for stripping into press flats, or direct-imaged plates for some presses. To determine which kind of output best suits your needs, talk with representatives from your service bureau and your book's printer.

Peripheral Hardware——Many pieces of equipment that attach to your computer can dramatically increase its power, its usefulness and its convenience to you and others involved with you as a self-publisher.

A *modem* enables you to transmit over telephone lines to other compatible computers electronic files of manuscript, graphics or both, combined into designed pages. This is very useful for receiving manuscripts from authors or editors and for transmitting typeset and designed pages to service bureaus. Sending materials by modem can speed up the publishing process dramatically by reducing to minutes or hours deliveries that easily would involve one or several days through the mail or other delivery services.

A *scanner* can allow you to take images, both drawings and photographs, into your computer for manipulation with various software——retouching, sizing, cropping, screening and importing the final image(s) into designed pages as graphic elements.

An *external disk drive* can greatly expand the capacity of your computer and your storage. Forty megabyte (or larger) external disks allow you to electronically store complete publications (even those including graphics that consume great amounts of electronic memory) outside your computer. That frees your computer's internal memory for live jobs.

Software——Four general types of software will interest you as a self-publisher——word processing, relational database, page design and makeup, and illustration. In general, more than one specific program is available for each application. The once clear-cut delineation between capabilities of these types of software is becoming fuzzy. The trend among software developers is to make all programs perform some key functions of others. A casual review of program descriptions in a software catalog quickly will reveal this. For example, even word processing programs allow you to do some fairly decent typesetting and multi-column page layout. And graphics programs allow you to enter text through them. This may serve you very well——you might be able to accomplish all your publishing prepress operations with one software program. This is significant since programs typically cost from a few hundred to several hundred dollars each. Your computer dealer, and magazines and catalogs about desktop publishing and personal computing will help you determine which program(s) can best suit your specific needs.*

Word Processing Three common word processing programs are WordPerfect, Word and Wordstar. As implied, this software is best suited for working with words. But the latest revisions of these programs incorporate many features of early graphics programs. So output from them can be graphically sophisticated.

Generally, however, you can think of word processing programs as turning your computer into a very sophisticated typewriter. End results often look much like a typewritten page. Word processing programs (because they are so universally used in so many busi-

---

*For descriptions of hundreds of programs and their applications, write or call for the latest edition of *MacWarehouse*, P.O. Box 3013, 1720 Oak Street, Lakewood, NJ 18701-3013, phone: 800-255-6227, fax: 908-905-9279.

nesses and homes) can be operated by many people. So manuscripts for books usually are created in a word processing program. Electronic files created with word processing programs can directly generate simple book pages. Or the files can be easily "poured" into page design programs, where different type styles can be assigned to the information, and the resulting type can be arranged into designed pages.

Relational Database   This type of program is ideal for creating publications that contain large volumes of information that is cross referenced, reorganized differently for various sections of a publication, and that may require frequent, even constant, updating. This kind of software would be ideal for parts and product catalogs, directories and the like. Two popular database programs are dBase that will run on PC and 4th Dimension for the Mac.

Besides being very efficient in maintaining large volumes of data and complex relationships among them, database programs allow writing rather sophisticated custom routines for outputting information in their records to pages that are graphically sophisticated and functional.

Page Design and Makeup   This software, through built-in "default" page design grids, allows the self-publisher to quickly and rather easily create professional-looking books. If none of the many standard grids available with a program suits your needs, it is not difficult to create and store custom page grids. You might use either standard or custom grids to create sophisticated publication design.

Though page design programs ordinarily permit direct entry of information into page layouts, a more common procedure is to pour or "import" word-processed files into these programs; then assign type styles, sizes and weights; then arrange the information on the page as desired. This sequence often is more efficient and less costly because it can use keystrokes created by typists or authors to generate type and pages. In addition, it dramatically reduces errors that inevitably creep in as manuscripts are re-keystroked for typesetting. As mentioned earlier, because of a broader use of word processing programs than design programs, more people know word processing than design programs.

Because design programs allow direct entry of information, corrections and changes can be efficiently entered directly into a designed page as late as minutes before creating final art or film that will be used to make plates for the press.

Three popular page design and makeup programs are Page-Maker, Quark Express and Ventura Publisher. Your software dealer can explain the advantages and disadvantages of each.

Illustration   These programs, though available to self-publishers with computer hardware, may not be practical. Not only does learning the software consume time; creating professional illustrations that are useful in publications will require conventional training in illustration and drawing, and an innate sense of esthetics within the user.

Illustration software can be used to create art ranging from charts and graphs to images that resemble sophisticated airbrushing or painting, as well as other techniques. Resulting images generally are imported through page design programs into spaces reserved for them in electronic page layouts. Then when the pages are output through high-end equipment at a service bureau, illustrations already are in place. If color has been used in the illustration, it can be automatically separated by the computer and output as separate film negatives----one for each color.

Some popular illustration programs include Adobe Illustrator, Aldus Freehand and Adobe Photoshop. Your software dealer can explain applications for each, as well as their advantages and disadvantages.

Composition

If you have decided to have your book set in type, the following will acquaint you with the typesetting capabilities available through various book printers. The most commonly used varieties of typesetting and composition are photocomposition, linotype and electronic typesetting.

You may discuss with your printer the different forms of composition and see what is available and the price ranges of each. Your printer should carefully analyze your manuscript for mixing of point size and fonts, column alignments, anticipated corrections and alterations, runarounds, line lengths, tables, formulas and footnotes. Only then will the printer be able to give you a realistic quote.

Photocomposition

The most sophisticated version of photocomposition now available is *computer-assisted photocomposition* (CAP). Images of the characters to be reproduced are electronically generated from the computerized instructions stored on magnetic disks. These images are formed on the face of a cathode ray tube, which is similar to a small television screen. The image is then focused onto photosensitive paper through a lens with the resulting exposure producing the desired characters. Corrections and alterations are made on a terminal that looks like a typewriter keyboard with a TV screen above it. If one character of one word (or multiples of either) are added, deleted or changed, only the affected words are involved. Other words around the change are not retyped. The terminal operator can visually verify that changes were correctly made before the page is produced or entered into the computer's memory.

When the finished manuscript is ready to be printed from within the memory banks, the typed characters are focused by a lens onto photosensitive paper at the rate of 600 per second. A frame holds the film or paper during exposure. A processor then develops, fixes and drys the photographic film or paper.

This method facilitates the changing and mixing of type styles. The computer can be programmed to produce complete pages with footnotes properly positioned. While the characters are still on the

84

screen, they can be expanded, condensed, obliqued (set in italics) or enlarged from 4-point type to 96-point type.

The input material is stored on magnetic tape. When it comes time to update or revise your manuscript for a second printing, only the new or corrected information is changed. The corrected tape is then run through the computer and photounit for automatic pagination (numbering of pages) and the generation of new, camera-ready copy. This revision capability is especially good for writers who will need to update their material frequently.

Another advantage of CAP is the capability to produce abridged versions or condensations of the original work. You can change the typefaces, layouts and point sizes easily.

CAP may seem a bit too technical for the average self-publisher, but it never hurts to know what is available.

Typesetting systems that yield galleys instead of made-up pages require a subsequent paste-up step to get to finished pages. Paste-up involves cutting galleys into page or column lengths and arranging type along with line stats and screened stats (or red window knockouts for halftones) into pages, and pasting everything in precise position onto boards which are photographed to make plate-ready negatives. These are stripped into flats and exposed onto press plates.

Linotype

The linotype machine carries the assembly of type one step further by casting an entire line as one unit. A solid slug of metal which contains all of the characters in a line is cast. It is proofed as in the monotype method, then the slugs are melted down for re-use.

In Figure 5.1, several of the most common typefaces used in books and for chapter headings and dust jackets are presented to give you an idea of the way they look and their corresponding sizes. This text is set in 12-point Palomino typeface, with 28-point Optima Extra Bold used for chapter titles, and 14- and 13-point Optima Extra Bold for subheads.

Figure 5.1 Sample Typefaces

ARIAL

ABCDEFGHIJKLMNOPQRSTUVWXYZ
abcdefghijklmnopqrstuvwxyz
1234567890
——/&?;:().,!$

Six-Point Alphabet

ABCDEFGHIJKLMNOPQRSTUVWXYZ

abcdefghijklmnopqrstuvwxyz

1234567890

—/&?;:().,!$

Seven-Point Alphabet

ABCDEFGHIJKLMNOPQRSTUVWXYZ

abcdefghijklmnopqrstuvwxyz

1234567890

——/&?;:().,!$

Eight-Point Alphabet

ABCDEFGHIJKLMNOPQRSTUVWXYZ

abcdefghijklmnopqrstuvwxyz

1234567890

——/&?;:().,!$

Nine-Point Alphabet

ABCDEFGHIJKLMNOPQRSTUVWXYZ

abcdefghijklmnopqrstuvwxyz

1234565780

—/&?;:().,!$

Figure 5.1 (continued)

OPTIMA

ABCDEFGHIJKLMNOPQRSTUVWXYZ
abcdefghijklmnopqrstuvwxyz
1234567890
------/&?;:().,!$

Six-Point Alphabet

ABCDEFGHIJKLMNOPQRSTUVWXYZ

abcdefghijklmnopqrstuvwxyz

1234567890

—/&?;:().,!$

Seven-Point Alphabet

ABCDEFGHIJKLMNOPQRSTUVWXYZ

abcdefghijklmnopqrstuvwxyz

1234567890

—/&?;:().,!$

Eight-Point Alphabet

ABCDEFGHIJKLMNOPQRSTUVWXYZ

abcdefghijklmnopqrstuvwxyz

1234567890

----/&?;:().,!$

Nine-Point Alphabet

ABCDEFGHIJKLMNOPQRSTUVWXYZ

abcdefghijklmnopqrstuvwxyz

1234567890

—/&?;:().,!$

Figure 5.1 Sample Typefaces (continued)

ROMAN

ABCDEFGHIJKLMNOPQRSTUVWXYZ
abcdefghijklmnopqrstuvwxyz
1234567890$

Six-Point Alphabet

How often do you stop short in the midst of talking or writing because you can't think of the right word? More often than you like to realize? It's embarrassing—and very annoying. The idea is clear in your mind. The word with the exact shade of meaning though, is of

abcdefghijklmnopqrstuvwxyz   1234567890$

ABCDEFGHIJKLMNOPQRSTUVWXYZ

Seven-Point Alphabet

How often to you stop short in the midst of talking or writing because you can't think of the right word? More often

than you like to realize? It's embarrassing—and very annoying. The idea is clear in your mind. The word with the exact

abcdefghijklmnopqrstuvwxyz   1234567890$

ABCDEFGHIJKLMNOPQRSTUVWXYZ

Eight-Point Alphabet

How often do you stop short in the midst of talking or writing because you can't think of the right word?

More often than you like to realize? It's embarrassing—and very annoying. The idea is clear in your mind.

abcdefghijklmnopqrstuvwxyz   1234567890$

ABCDEFGHIJKLMNOPQRSTUVWXYZ

Nine-Point Alphabet

How often do you stop short in the midst of talking or writing because you can't think of the

right word? More often than you like to realize? It's embarrassing—and very annoying. The

idea

abcdefghijklmnopqrstuvwxyz   1234567890$

ABCDEFGHIJKLMNOPQRSTUVWXYZ

Figure 5.1 (continued)

TIMES NEW ROMAN

ABCDEFGHIJKLMNOPQRSTUVWXYZ
abcdefghijklmnopqrstuvwxyz
1234567890$

Six-Point Alphabet

How often do you stop short in the midst of talking or writing because you can't think of the right word? More often than you like to realize? It's em-

barrassing—and very annoying. The idea is clear in your mind. The word with the exact shade of meaning though, is of

abcdefghijklmnopqrstuvwxyz   1234567890$

ABCDEFGHIJKLMNOPQRSTUVWXYZ

Seven-Point Alphabet

How often do you stop short in the midst of talking or writing because you can't think of the right word? More often than you

like to realize? It's embarrassing—and very annoying. The idea is clear in your mind. The

abcdefghijklmnopqrstuvwxyz   1234567890$

ABCDEFGHIJKLMNOPQRSTUVWXYZ

Eight-Point Alphabet

How often do you stop short in the midst of talking or writing because you can't think of the right word? More

often than you like to realize? It's embarrassing—and very annoying. The idea

abcdefghijklmnopqrstuvwxyz   1234567890$

ABCDEFGHIJKLMNOPQRSTUVWXYZ

Nine-Point Alphabet

How often do you stop short in the midst of talking or writing because you can't think of the right

word? More often than you like to realize? It's embarrassing—and very annoying.

abcdefghijklmnopqrstuvwxyz   1234567890$

ABCDEFGHIJKLMNOPQRSTUVWXYZ

The typefaces and point size examples in Figure 5.1 are only commonly used examples of the hundreds of different typefaces available. Take this book with you when you go to your printer, and discuss their availability. Your printer may offer other typefaces that are not pictured here.

If you are not sure about what point size you will need, remember that any book can be made to appear larger or smaller, depending on your needs. This is true in most cases, regardless of the size of your manuscript. Tell the printer approximately how many finished pages you have in mind, and he or she will be able to calculate the point size, leading and other requirements needed to produce a book of the desired size from the manuscript.

Of course, you don't make a 100-page manuscript a thick book the size of *War and Peace*, but within reason these elements of composition are quite flexible.

For an excellent discussion on how to design with and specify type, see *Designing with Type: A Basic Course in Typography* by James Craig and Susan B. Meyer. It is published by Watson-Guptill Publications.

Methods of Printing

Major new developments have been made in the book printing industry in recent years, paralleling the progress made in computers and composition techniques. Following are a few examples of the most modern printing methods available today.

The first is the *belt press book production system*. This allows books to be printed by starting with rolled stock (paper) on one end and the delivery of completed books at the other. The books are formed with adhesive bindings. This means that books are printed, bound, covered and trimmed, and the best press can produce up to 200 books per minute.

The belt press book production system is considered to be the most versatile, economical production system for one-color workbooks, textbooks, paperbacks and hardcover books. It is essentially a single-color, perfecting web letterpress that is linked to an adhesive binding line. Its unique features are the flexible page plates mounted on variable length belts. This permits printing the entire book at one time. Also unique are the sequential slitting, folding and collating operations that convert the printed web into a gathered book ready for adhesive binding. Combined, this becomes a book production system capable of completing up to 200 books per minute and delivers both completed paperbacks and adhesive bound books that are ready for hard covers.

How It Works—— The flexible plates are mounted on two belts, one for printing each side of the web, with the pages imposed to print head to foot, giving a correct grain book. As each side of the web is printed, it is passed through driers. Next, it is slit into ribbons one page wide or two pages wide (depending on the number of pages imposed across the web). The two-page ribbons pass over an individual former and are folded into a one-page-wide ribbon (which is called a four-page signature). One-page-wide ribbons go directly from slitting to the cut-off unit.

All ribbons are then collected, one on top of the other, and enter the cut-off unit where the ribbons are cut into signatures. The signatures are collected into complete books on the forks of a vertical collating unit.

The collated books are then transported on a conveyor into an adhesive binding line. After binding, the books receive either preprinted paper covers or endsheets.* After the books leave the binder, they are conveyed to a three-knife trimmer where they are trimmed on three sides.

Books to be casebound** are stacked on pallets and transported to the "casing-in" department. Books which have paper covers are

---

* *Endsheets* are the blank pages between a book's cover and text.

complete at this point and are packed in cartons or stacked on pallets for shipment.

Typefaces Most Suitable Baskerville, 8-point and above; Caledonia, 8-point and above; Caslon, 8-point and above; Caslon Old Face, 10-point and above; Century Expanded; Electra, 10-point and above; Garamond #3, 10-point and above; Granjon, 10-point and above; Ionic; Janson; Old Style #1, 9-point and above; Old Style #7; Primer; Times Roman, 8-point and above.

Trim Sizes Trim sizes are infinitely variable in width across the web between the minimum of 4½ inches and the maximum of 8¾ inches. For head-to-foot dimension along the web, the press cut-off can be adjusted to quarter-inch increments from 6 inches to 11¾.

Figure 5.2 is a diagram that illustrates the belt press production system.

Figure 5.2 Belt Press Production System

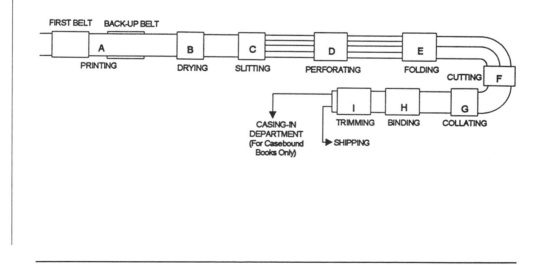

** *Casebound* books are hardcover books.

Sheet Fed Offset

A second method of printing is called *sheet fed offset lithography*. The system is used primarily for short-to-medium, black-and-white or color runs. The individual sheets are fed through the presses, and the printed product is delivered at the other end. Each sheet is as good as the one before it, and identical.

These presses (if perfectors) print both sides of the press sheet simultaneously, so up to 128 pages (at approximately 6 x 9-inch trim) can be printed in one pass through the press. Since the feeders on these presses can be adapted to paper stock in rolls, a great amount of money can be saved when purchasing paper. Rolls of paper are usually much cheaper than sheets for longer press runs.

Typical products may range from those requiring limited (or no) halftones (photographs or art) to those requiring fine-quality reproduction of single-color halftones, duotones and four-color separations. Typical products on the low end might be adult trade books, elementary/high school and college texts, dictionaries, professional books (law, business, medicine), technical and scientific reference works and a large percentage of the scholarly titles published by university presses. On the high end would be products such as art books requiring faithful reproduction of paintings, and photographs.

Web Offset

Web offset lithography is usually reserved for press runs of 3,000 and up, but due to its versatility, economies can be vast. The web presses are used for any book or catalog, and for both color and black-and-white printing. The same type of press that prints one-color bibles on lightweight paper can also deliver six-color pictorials on heavily enameled stock. In various configurations of from two to six units, this press category has the back-up capacity to protect the production run.

M-1000 web presses are commonly used by many commercial printers, and they are comprised of as many as six in-line printing units. Each unit simultaneously prints one color on each side of the web. Various color and paging combinations are arrived at by using multiple units. It is possible to achieve interweaving on one-and-a-half or two webs to result in different two-color and four-color combinations.

The printing "plates" are actually cylinders that operate as impression cylinders on each other, allowing for printing on both sides of the web at once. Since each unit runs two plates, one on each side of the web, a total of 12 plates are used when perfecting six units.

The M-1000 web press is capable of delivering almost any size book. The *tabloid fold* is the largest signature produced on this press, and it can go up to 11¾ x 19 inches before trimming. One web produces an eight-page signature, and two webs produce a 16-page signature. See Figure 5.3 for an illustration of this method.

Figure 5.3 Tabloid Fold Products

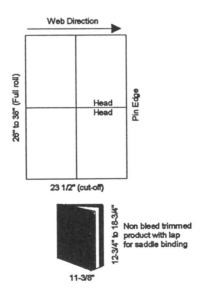

Chopper fold books on the M-1000 press are very popular for commercial printing, as well as book printing, because the signatures delivered are catalog size. (See Figure 5.4.)

Figure 5.4 Chopper Fold Products

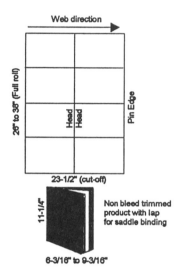

To simplify the explanation of the printing process somewhat, the printing of a book usually involves taking a photograph of the material to be produced. For example, to reproduce a typed page by photo offset, the printer shoots a negative of the page. It will reproduce only in 100 percent black (the type) and 100 percent white (all the space not covered by type). This is called a *line shot*.

The photo negative is made to the desired size of the final product. That is, it is possible to enlarge the negative in proportion to its original size. Let's say that you want to reproduce an 8½ x 11 inch page. The negative is made to 8½ x 11 inches and is transferred to a paper, plastic or metal printing plate that bears a light-sensitive emulsion coating. Thus the negative image becomes positive on the plate. Mounted on an offset press, this right-reading positive plate transfers ink it picks up from inking rollers to the blanket on an impression cylinder, which then lays the image down onto paper.

In addition to the *line* or solid black-and-white subject, printers make *halftones* that, when viewed from normal reading distance, create the illusion of continuous tones from black through a range of gray to white. The ink fountain of an offset press carries ink of a single color, which often is black. Printing is a simple all-or-nothing situation. A press can either put ink on paper or not. To create the illusion of printing continuous tones (black through grays to white), as generally is desired when reproducing a photograph, a halftone screen is sandwiched in contact with a sheet of film in a process camera back. That camera is used to rephotograph the original image through that screen. When the exposure is made, the resulting negative consists of thousands of tiny clear or opaque dots of varying sizes. The halftone screen (similar to a window screen) is made up of tiny individual square, elliptical or round dots. Each dot can be totally filled with ink or totally empty. The illusion of gray, from normal reading distance, is created by the eye merging together these dots that result from the halftone-making process.

Photographs: How They Are Printed

If you have photographs to be reproduced in your book, your printer will have the picture "screened" and show you proofs indicating how they will reproduce in the finished book.

With the addition of photographs, the plate-making process is not necessarily more complicated. The screened photos (halftones) must be combined with the type (or line copy) in the same positions they will occupy on the finished page. They are "stripped" together with type pages and other graphic elements into a *flat*. The flat is the paper matrix with holes cut in where the line and halftone copy appear. The actual printing plate is made by exposing the plate's light-sensitive surface through the holes in the flat.

Printing It Yourself

There is still another avenue of printing open to the self-publishing author if you feel that the foregoing is a bit over your head at this point. That avenue is doing the whole job yourself.

Before rushing out to purchase a four-color press, however, bear in mind that without a large capital outlay and considerable talent, printing is always best left in the hands of a professional. If your book is to consist of text only and the material lends itself to a simple binding method (such as loose-leaf, GBC, spiral, tape or saddle stitch), then do-it-yourself printing is a reasonable alternative. Such a procedure also allows for additional sales of updated information to a prime audience---your previous customers.

The Kitchen Table Printing Press

An acquaintance of mine began a "kitchen table" publishing venture a few years ago that provided him with a comfortable income while attending law school. Before deciding on law for his career, he had wanted to be a doctor. Upon applying to medical schools in this country, he found only closed doors. One of his friends told him that many medical schools overseas had vacancies.

Despite my friend's change in vocations from medicine to law, he learned a great deal about medical school vacancies abroad. In what proved to be a wise entrepreneurial decision, he decided to share his knowledge with other prospective medical students by publishing a book on the subject.

As a student, he did not have sufficient capital to pay to have his book published, and he was the type of individual who enjoyed doing things for himself. That combination of ingredients motivated him to buy a multilith press (generally considered "duplicator" quality) capable of handling a standard 8½ x 11 inch sheet. He typed directly onto paper masters (printing plates) that attached to the press.

More practical today would be to invest in computer hardware (equipment) and software (complex electronic instructions that tell that equipment what to do) to generate professional graphics, set type and/or produce camera-ready pages, then have the book commercially printed. A book created and stored on computer disk allows frequent updates at low cost compared to having to key-stroke again an entire book or substantial portions of it.

The book production process for our student became a family affair, with his wife punching holes in the sheets and assembling them in proper order while he printed. The final steps of assembling them into three-holed binders were accomplished together. They were then shipped out.

Probably as practical today would be to run this kind of book on a high-speed photocopier that can tape bind in line. Available through most copy shops, this method is practical for short-run books. It is fast, professional in appearance and relatively low cost per unit. It allows for on-demand production.

My friend was able to advertise his service by posting inexpensive notices on school bulletin boards. His operation was simple and did not require any greater degree of sophistication than he was able to lend to it.

We have deliberately set this page
in standard typewriter style to illustrate
the way in which you may prepare your
final manuscript. Whether you are simply
preparing the manuscript for your printer
(where it will be typeset) or plan to
reproduce typewritten pages, this is the
format that is most common.

Notice the margins on this page.
These are standard. This page is double
spaced and was typed on an IBM-compatible
computer using a standard typewriter
Courier typeface.

There is a wide variety of type
sizes and styles available when using a
computer or an IBM Selectric typewriter.
These machines are available for sale,
lease and rent from authorized agents, who
may be found in the Yellow Pages.

This is what the same type looks like
with elite spacing.

Types of Binding

There are several different types of book binding. Each binding type offers different degrees of durability, ease of opening and the ability to lay flat. The costs vary with the amount of labor and materials required for each.

Smyth Sewn Hardcover Books—These books are bound by a thread that passes through the backbone fold line of each signature to the adjacent signature. The operator feeds signatures from a stack of gathered books one at a time into the machine. This automatically sews them in the gathered order. Controlled by foot pedals, the machine also pastes the first and last sections to the adjacent signatures and cuts the threads between books. Sewing is a relatively expensive operation with a high labor cost. Therefore, it is usually reserved for the highest quality books.

Figure 5.5 is an illustration of the Smyth Sewn method.

Figure 5.5 Smyth Sewn Binding

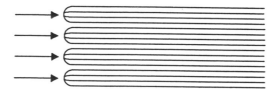

Smyth Sewn Softcover Books—This method is identical to the one for hardcover books, and the only cost savings will be in the cheaper softcover paper stock.

Adhesive Bound Hardcover Books—In this method, a stretch paper is wrapped around the backbone and secured with adhesive to gain additional strength for what are sometimes referred to as the endpapers in the casing-in operation.

In an adhesive bound book, the pages are held together by a flexible adhesive. The glues that are used have been specifically formulated to provide strength and resiliency over a long period of time. Significant advances in adhesive technology have been made in recent years, resulting in greatly improved binding quality. During the binding operation, the backbone of the signatures must be milled away to allow the adhesive to adhere securely to the inner pages of the signature. This binding facilitates the inclusion of inserts, color sections, etc. between signatures. Figure 5.6 is an illustration of adhesive bound book binding.

Figure 5.6 Adhesive Binding

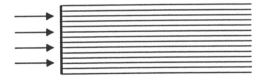

Adhesive Bound Softcover Books—This is identical to adhesive bound hardcover books. The soft wraparound cover is applied while the book is on the binder. The complete book—pages and cover—is trimmed and may be packed immediately.

Side Wire Stitch Hardcover Books—This method is sometimes also referred to as *side sewn* or *McCain binding*. In these methods, the signatures are laid on top of each other in proper order. Wire stitches or staples or threads are passed through the thickness of the book, front to back, to hold all signatures together. Since needle and thread are used in side sewn binding, the thickness is more limited than with side wire stitching. Side stitch and side sewn bindings facilitate the addition of inserts and color sections but will not lay flat. Figure 5.7 is an illustration of this method.

Figure 5.7 Side Wire Stitch and/or Side Sewn (McCain) Binding

Side Wire Stitch Softcover Books—This is identical to the same method for hardcover books. What savings you might realize would come from using a soft paper cover rather than a hardback.

Saddle Stitch Books—Saddle stitch binding is widely used in the publications industry. Most magazines are produced with saddle stitch binding. The signatures are progressively inserted inside each other, with or without a separate four-page cover. The signatures are fastened together along the backbone fold with wire staples. The product is usually trimmed on three sides in a web press in one operation, and in most cases is limited to about ⅜ inch in total thickness or bulk. Figure 5.8 is an illustration of the saddle stitch method.

Figure 5.8 Saddle Stitch Binding

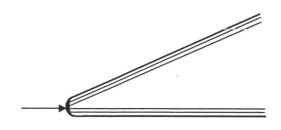

For economical book production, trimmed page sizes within the normal range should be used. Examples of normal range sizes are:

6 x 9 inches
5½ x 8½ inches
7 x 10 inches
8½ x 11 inches

Binding Style Characteristics

Binding	Durability	Relative Cost	Ability to Lay Flat	Ease of Opening
Smyth Sewn Hardcover	Excellent	High	Excellent	Very Good
Smyth Sewn Softcover	Very Good	High	Excellent	Very Good
Adhesive Hardcover	Good	Low	Good	Good
Adhesive Softcover	Fair	Low	Good	Good
Side Wire Stitch Hardcover	Excellent	Medium	Fair	Fair
Side Wire Stitch Softcover	Good	Medium	Fair	Fair
Side Sewn Hardcover	Excellent	High	Fair	Good
Saddle Stitch	Fair	Low	Very Good	Excellent

Binding Style Characteristics (cont.)

Binding	Minimum Size	Maximum Size	Minimum Thickness	Maximun Thickness
Smyth Sewn Hardcover	4" x 6"	10" x 14"	1/4"	2-1/2"
Smyth Sewn Softcover	4" x 6"	10" x 14"	1/4"	2-1/2"
Adhesive Hardcover	4" x 6"	10" x 14"	1/4"	2-1/2"
Adhesive Softcover	4" x 6"	11" x 16"	1/4"	2-1/2"
Side Wire Stitch Hardcover	5" x 7"	9" x 12"	1/4"	2-1/4"
Side Wire Stitch Softcover	5" x 7"	9" x 12"	1/4"	2-1/4"
Side Sewn Hardcover	4" x 6"	10" x 14"	3/8"	2"
Saddle Stitch	3-3/8" x 8"	11-3/4" x 18-3/4	none	9/16"

Illustrations----An Important Asset

Writers sometimes tend to think that books should have words only and leave the photographs and other art to the magazines. For a novel, I would probably agree. But other books, particularly "how-to's," can benefit greatly from the use of illustrations. Those on travel, beauty, exercise and many other self-help subjects would suffer without photographs to clearly define just what the writer is setting out to explain.

If you doubt this, try writing instructions for performing a slightly complicated exercise or building/construction process. Sometimes, no matter how good you are at explaining yourself, it is impossible to get across the exact meaning of your words without an accompanying photograph or drawing.

If you feel your book would benefit by including photographs, you are immediately confronted with the problem of where to obtain them. Here is a list of 10 places where you can start.

Sources of Illustrations

1. Create photographs or art yourself if you're competent with the technique.
2. You can hire freelance photographers and artists.
3. Prowl the libraries, art galleries and museums. Many have Ektachrome transparencies of paintings and exhibits for free use. Under the new copyright law, however, you must obtain permission to use these photographs. You must get this permission from the copyright owner, usually the creator.
4. Turn to other publications for help, either on a free or paid basis.
5. Buy from photograph syndicates or supply houses that sell "stock" photographs. One-time stock rates for color images usually are negotiable, but the low end ranges from $200 to $1,000 and more. Price varies drastically depending upon

your publication's press run and the size you intend to reproduce the image.

6. Seek assistance from your local Chamber of Commerce, city or county government.

7. Check professional, trade and industry associations for the possiblity of no-cost photographs and drawings.

8. Private companies, usually through their public relations departments, will often provide free photos.

9. Contact government sources. Perhaps the Department of Agriculture, for example, would have photographs for gardening subjects.

10. You can keep an eye open for photographers who might appear at an event you are attending. Get their names, ask to see the results and offer to buy their photographs if they meet your requirements.

Taking Your Own Photographs

It is recommended that you limit your photography to be included in your book to black-and-white unless the subject specifically warrants the additional expense of four-color printing. The reason for this is that four-color printing costs about four times as much as black-and-white. Of course, if your subject is fine art, sculpture, travel or color photography, you might have to have four-color printing.

If you are not an accomplished photographer, I suggest that you enroll in an inexpensive course at your local YMCA, high school, community group or college. This will give you the basics you must know in order to select a good camera, set up your shots, and the various processes to develop and print your own photographs. Processing black-and-white film and creating prints from the negatives, though enjoyable, may be best left to labs that service professionals. The process requires equipment that can cost several hundred dollars or more, and learning to produce images of reproduction quality can take several months of study and practice.

If you are serious about top quality photography in your book, buy or rent a 35mm single lens reflex (SLR) camera. Your local camera shop will be able to assist you. Often the employees are knowledgeable and willing to answer questions.

Buying a Camera

Buy the best camera you can afford. Or try renting several demonstration models before deciding on the best one for you. Avoid box cameras, subminiatures or stereos. Instamatics or pocket cameras just don't have the focus or light metering flexibility you will need for professional-looking photographs. The negatives yielded by pocket cameras are not large enough or of high enough quality to be satisfactorily enlarged.

Elements of a Good Photo

Your pictures should look professional rather than like snapshots. Here are a few pointers when taking pictures of your own and in selecting other photos for possible inclusion in your book:

1. Avoid clutter and distracting elements that pull the eye from the main point.
2. Try for contrast in pattern and tonal shades.
3. Seek action, either obvious or implied.
4. Tell a story. Remember that even a portrait can tell a story—a smile, a scowl, an intense expression, a disdainful mood or a serious expression.
5. Shoot for the unusual.
6. Seek human interest, feeling and emotion in your subjects.
7. Strive for technical excellence in focus, exposure and development.

Handling Photographs

As a final note on using photographs in your book, don't ruin an otherwise suitable picture by handling it carelessly. Here are some pointers to help prevent any deterioration in quality:

- Keep surfaces clean.

- Avoid using paper clips, writing in pen or lead pencil on the backs of photos, or bearing down too heavily on overlays. These actions can crack the emulsion and ruin the print.

- Keep pictures flat and use stiffeners.

- Hold retouching and airbrushing to a minimum, and then have it done professionally.

- Mark cropping instructions clearly. *Cropping* refers to marking a photograph to exclude unnecessary or distracting background. There generally are two acceptable ways to indicate cropping on a print: 1) grease pencil tic marks in a photo's white borders; 2) tissue overlay with the area of the photograph you want to reproduce precisely outlined on the overlay with a fine-tip water-base marker (an alcohol marker might easily bleed through your overlay and damage the photograph).

- Carefully guard both negatives and your last print. File by processing or negative number, subject, issue or article in a system that permits easy reference and quick reproduction of new prints from the old negative.

Line Drawings

Line drawings are another good way to illustrate your book without the expense of photographs. I suggest you have drawings prepared by a commercial artist because quality is most important.

I've designed a simple questionnaire (see Figure 5.9) to help you better plan your books, as well as a worksheet (see Figure 5.10) to prepare you to discuss it with your printer.

Figure 5.9 Questionnaire

Which Method Is Best for You?

Your Book:

1a. Number of characters in manuscript_____

1b. Information is available on computer disk: [ ] No

                                                       [ ] Yes

                Program _____

                Revision # _____

                Operating System (hardware) _____

2. Additional pages (title page, copyright page, dedication page, acknowledgments, table of contents, foreword, preface, index, glossary, suggested readings, bibliography, endnotes) _____

3. Number of pages containing tables, graphs or charts_____

4. Number of pages containing halftones _____

5. Number of pages containing four-color photographs or illustrations_____

6. Approximate number of words in manuscript (total of all pages) _____

7. Type size used for manuscript _____ pica _____ elite

8. Type of composition desired

                [ ] typewritten

                [ ] laser printer output

                [ ] service bureau output from desktop publishing files

                [ ] commercial quality typesetting

Figure 5.9 (continued)

9. Typeface desired for text _____

        9a. Type point size _____

        9b. Line leading _____

        9c. Line length (picas) _____

10. Typeface desired for chapter headings _____

11. Typeface desired for cover/dust jacket _____

    _____

12. Method of printing desired _____

13. Method of binding desired_____

14. Jacket _____yes _____no

15. Graphic artwork desired _____

    _____

16. Paper

    16a. Cover: Weight _____

                     Name_____

                     Color _____

    16b. Text: Weight _____

                     Name_____

                     Color _____

17. Items to discuss further with printer _____

    _____

    _____

    _____

    _____

Figure 5.10 Worksheet

Comparing Quotes from Printers

Specification	Company A	Company B	Company C
Typesetting costs	_____	_____	_____
Prepress costs	_____	_____	_____

Including: _____ Square-cut halftones (number)

_____ Four-color separations (number)

	Company A	Company B	Company C
Paper costs	_____	_____	_____
Printing costs	_____	_____	_____
Binding costs	_____	_____	_____
Shipping costs	_____	_____	_____
# of copies in 1st run	_____	_____	_____

Divide all costs by a per-thousand figure to arrive at your unit cost per book. For instance, if you are planning a 5,000-book first printing, divide all costs by 5,000 to determine your cost per book, and enter below.

Cost per copy (1st run)	_____	_____	_____

Cost per thousand to reprint (from standing film)

_____   _____   _____

Chapter 6

Ways To Sell Your Book

I'm willing to bet that the world's greatest book was either never published at all or was never promoted enough to sell out of its first printing. Having owned a publishing company for 20 years, I am intimately aware of the unmined "gold" lying around in the form of unpublished manuscripts and poorly promoted books. This is why an author's old works are often dredged up, given cosmetic changes and republished when he or she connects with a winner. Suddenly, all manuscripts that were rejected and all the books that died because of low-key promotion are hot properties.

The feature which makes this book unique is our formula for creating a *bestseller*. The key word here is *seller*. What you want to do now is to connect with that *one* book and let your future successes flow naturally from that.

With the information discussed so far in this book, you have the knowledge to get your manuscript into print at the least cost and maximum effectiveness. In itself, this will separate you from the gloomy side of the next batch of statistics:

In the U.S. only about 3,000 authors are in the elite group whose books sell out of their first printings.

This is where this book can really help you.

Your Selling Game Plan

Now that you have chosen a bestselling subject and tested it, have gone through the necessary steps to get your manuscript into print and have protected your investment, you are ready to develop a marketing "game plan."

It has been my experience that the best method of merchandising a book to bestseller status is through direct response selling. It is the best way to reach a large number of potential buyers at the lowest cost. Inherent in the success of direct response business is an effective advertising plan.

While Madison Avenue executives have built the image of advertising into frighteningly complex proportions, it's really a simple process.

Writing Ads That Sell

How do you write an advertisement that will cause people to order your book? Here is my approach:

1. Before writing your advertisement, make a list of every benefit you can think of to your readers. Don't write down the reasons why *you* like it. Give reasons why someone else should buy it and how it will help him or her. Reread each page, and write down each benefit.
2. Get readers' attention. Use a powerful *headline*. The headline is often two-thirds of an ad's success. The best headline is often the very biggest benefit a reader gets from your book.
3. Hold their attention. Use subheads or illustrations. Your first paragraph is crucial.
4. Tell a full and complete story. Use every sales appeal that space will permit. Pile up benefits to the customer. You can

easily tire of the complete story, but new readers have never heard it. Use every bit of space as effectively as you can.

5. Use testimonials. Make it believable. Use specific figures, guarantees, reviewer comments and endorsements.
6. Prove the book is a bargain. Build up the value to readers. Make people believe that the information in your book is really worth four times the price they will pay for it.
7. Make it easy to buy by telling how to go about it. Provide a response device (coupon) or clear instructions for ordering.
8. Give a reason to buy *now*. Use special offers and various rewards for promptness.

These techniques have been used not only by me but also by the most successful direct response advertisers in the world. They are the "Eight Basic Truths" in the advertising industry. If you abide by them, you greatly enhance the odds of an ad's success.

Other considerations also go into the make-up of an advertisement. One factor is the size of the ad. Another is the media you select in which to place your advertisement.

(Note: I also currently conduct marketing seminars that teach you how to write ads that sell. If you want to learn more about writing successful ads, you may write or call Nicholas Direct for a schedule.)

Classified Advertisements

As mentioned earlier, classified advertisements are probably the best place to start. They are inexpensive. And you are not risking thousands of dollars in an untested ad or media. Keep the "Truths" in mind and the ad will be far superior even though by its nature a classified ad has more limited room than a larger space ad.

You must capture attention. In a classified ad, boxed into a column with hundreds of other competing ads, this is vitally important. Figure 6.1 is an example of one of the first classified ads for my first book.

Figure 6.1 Classified Ad----1¼"

~~~~~~~~~~~~~~~~~~~~~~~~~~
BUSINESS SERVICES
~~~~~~~~~~~~~~~~~~~~~~~~~~

**HOW TO FORM YOUR OWN
CORPORATION WITHOUT A
LAWYER FOR UNDER $50.**

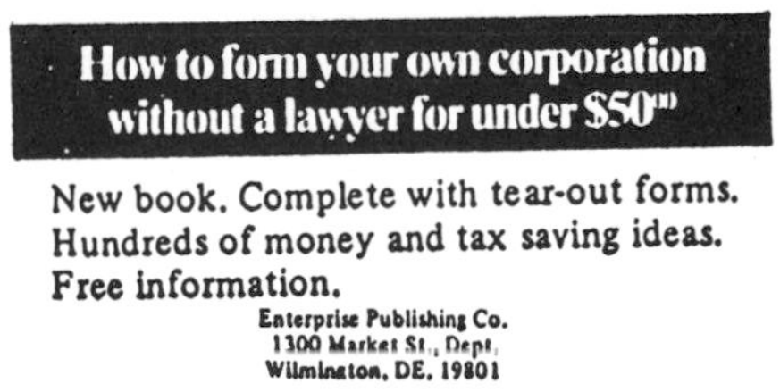

New book. Complete with tearout
forms. Hundreds of money and tax
saving ideas. Send for free information. Enterprise Publishing Co.
1300 Market St., Dept.
Wilmington, DE. 19801
~~~~~~~~~~~~~~~~~~~~~~~~~~

Figure 6.2 shows you a small display advertisement, which was slightly more expensive but pulled even greater response.

Figure 6.2 Small Display Ad----2¼" x ⅞"

**How to form your own corporation
without a lawyer for under $50"**

New book. Complete with tear-out forms.
Hundreds of money and tax saving ideas.
Free information.
Enterprise Publishing Co.
1300 Market St., Dept.
Wilmington, DE. 19801

I then started advertising the book directly, rather than having the customer write for more information. A coupon appeared in the next ad (see Figure 6.3).

Figure 6.3 Display Ad—2" x 2¾"

And that worked so well that I decided to make the ads bigger and tell more of the story (see Figure 6.4).

Figure 6.4 One-Third Page Ad—Double-Column Format 4⅝"x 4⅞"

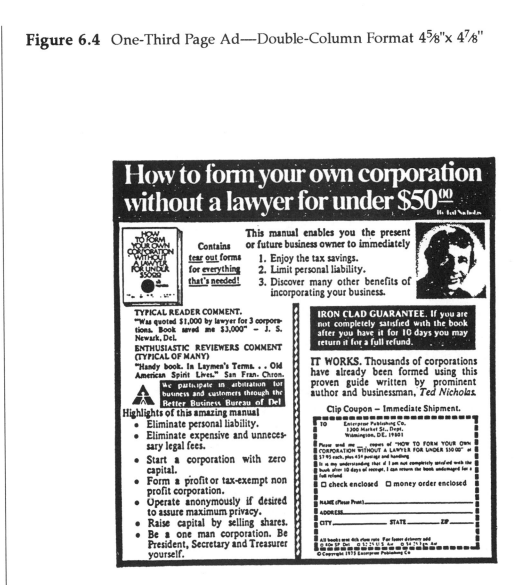

Figure 6.5 One-Third Page----Single-Column Format 2¼" x 10"

Then I ran the first full-page ad.

Figure 6.6 Full-Page Ad

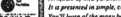

Direct Mail

The same rules used in space advertising apply to *direct mail*. You send a letter to the recipient offering them the opportunity to purchase your book. The "package" includes an order card, a business reply envelope (BRE) and sometimes a brochure about your book. Whatever you can fit into an envelope that will keep it under the current weight limit for first class mail or third class mail——and that sells——should go into a direct mail letter.

If your letter, BRE, brochure and order card (when inserted in the mailing envelope) weigh just over the weight limit, add more information until it weighs just under the next higher weight limit. Personal experience has shown that the more you tell a potential customer about your product, the better the response will be. So include all the information you can at the lowest mailing cost.

The Mailing List

A direct mail letter is designed to go unsolicited to a name you have rented in the form of prospective buyers. Lists of names are available by customer category from mailing list brokers. These are supplied for a fee of $50 to $100 per thousand names. You can get a list of people who have purchased vegetable seeds by mail during the last year or a list of people who recently bought retirement property and might be good candidates for a gardening book. A conversation with a representative of a good mail list company mentioned later in this book might reveal categories of potential customers who would not occur to you.

The Direct Mail Letter

Follow all the suggestions in the "Eight Basic Truths." Direct mail is more flexible than space advertising because you have more room. You are not limited in special dimensions. You can have a four-page letter or as little as a single page of copy. Again, the more you tell, the more people will order your product.

120

The Order Card

The order card is of utmost importance. People sometimes do not read your letter and instead look at the order card first to determine what the offer is and how much it costs. The order card is a critical element in your direct mail package for this reason. It must restate the offer in compelling terms, give the price, detailed ordering instructions and provide the opportunity to get in your last sales effort. People want convenience in ordering your product. If they have to go through a lot of rigamarole, they will get aggravated and toss your direct mail package. Make it easy to order.

Here is a sample order coupon:

> Yes! I definitely want to find out how I can save from $300 to $2,500 in legal fees when incorporating. Send me your book, *How To Form Your Own Corporation Without a Lawyer for under $75* immediately. I am enclosing my __check __money order for ___ copies, in the amount of $ _____.

The Brochure

You might want to also enclose a sales brochure. This enables people to skim the offer quickly without reading the letter. I've had great success with a four-page brochure. It is printed on both sides of an 11 x 17-inch sheet, then folded in half to measure 8½ x 11 inches. The brochure information follows the formula for a full-page advertisement and incorporates much of the same information. You can never tell if your recipient is going to read all the elements in the direct mail package. Assume that he or she will be reading only one of them. Don't worry about repeating copy elements----as sometimes just the letter, the brochure or the order card is read. The more often you emphasize the benefits of ordering your book in different formats, the more orders you will receive.

Using Color

To set the brochure off from the letter, use a colored stock. Use two ink colors on a colored or buff background. This gives the impression and interest of full color at lower cost. In reality, this is a two-color printing job, black and another color. In quantities of 5,000, this type of brochure costs about 20 cents a piece. If you need more information about your book to put into the brochure, reprint the table of contents. This is very effective because it gives your reader a clear idea of exactly what your book covers. Figure 6.7 is an example of a successful brochure.

Figure 6.7 Sample Successful Brochure

Figure 6.7 (continued)

 ENTERPRISE • DEARBORN
520 North Dearborn Street
Chicago, Illinois 60610-4354

BULK RATE
U.S. POSTAGE
PAID
DEARBORN FINANCIAL
PUBLISHING, INC.

ENTERPRISE • DEARBORN recycles.
Please recycle this catalog after ordering.

FREE BOOK! | **A WORRY-FREE RETIREMENT**

Imagine having no money worries during your retirement. You could locate where you'd really want to live, have the home of your dreams, purchase a beautiful, new car every year, and travel whenever and wherever you want to go.

Michael Leonetti, the nation's premier retirement planner, has written a book that shows you how, step-by-step.

It's never too late. Nor too early. You'll be guided toward a retirement of ease. Live the lifestyle you choose. Best of all, the time-tested and proven financial strategies will require very little of your time.

But, you must plan properly so that your move into retirement is a smooth transition from your working years, rather than a shock.

You'll get hands on help with this 262-page book packed with over 80 pages of forms, checklists, resources and practical tips.

This book will motivate you to look forward to the retirement years and be able to do all the things you've always wanted to do.

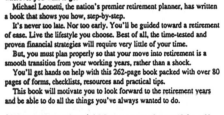

Catalog #5608-10   Price: $19.95

When you order $100 or more from this all-new and expanded Enterprise•Dearborn catalog, you will receive a free copy (normally $19.95) of the best-selling RETIRE WORRY-FREE: FINANCIAL STRATEGIES FOR TOMORROW'S INDEPENDENCE.

Figure 6.7 Sample Successful Brochure (continued)

II. The Growing Business

What Will You Do When Your Personal Assets are Seized to Satisfy a Judgment Against Your Corporation?

"All the forms your small business corporation will ever need, already written for you! This book takes the 'mystery' out of corporate law, and puts the money back into your account."
— AMA Book Club

Fully Revised and Updated!

Also Available on Computer Diskette! See Column 3 for details...

Book Only—
Catalog # 5615-06   Price: $69.95

Diskette Only—   Price: $69.95
   IBM and Compatibles:
     5 1/4" Catalog #5615-10
     3 1/2" Catalog # 5615-11

Book/Diskette Set—Price: $99.90
   IBM and Compatibles:
     5 1/4" Catalog # 5615-07
     3 1/2" Catalog # 5615-08

Beware! All your many tax benefits of owning a corporation could be wiped out overnight!

How? The IRS could visit you and claim you have not kept proper corporate minutes. Just like that, you could lose the very same tax benefits which prompted you to form a corporation from the start.

While incorporating entitles you to tax and other benefits (including the all-important limited liability), you are required in return to follow specific reporting and recording rules, or these wonderful benefits can be whisked away — right when you need them most.

Why Bother with Corporate Recordkeeping? After all, it seems downright silly (especially for small, even one-person corporations) to keep records of stockholder meetings and board of director's meetings...adopting resolutions...isn't it all just a waste of time?

Well, just ask any of the thousands of entrepreneurs who have lost fortunes because they failed to keep adequate records. You should look at corporate recordkeeping this way: It's part of the price you pay to get the tax benefits and personal protections granted to you through your corporation.

Recordkeeping— Demanded by Those You Depend On. And if you ever need to raise capital—even a simple loan from the bank—you're required to get properly notarized authorizations. Banks, insurance companies and state and federal agencies require notarized authorizations to grant loans, buy property and equipment, enter into leases and even sell assets. The small business owner simply has no option but to "get it in writing."

The forms go on and on...and because the IRS doesn't make anything easy, you'll need, at minimum, a dozen or more documents to keep your corporation alive and functioning for just one year.

How do you get this accomplished? Lawyers. Yes, you can hire a lawyer, like the big companies do, and pay $100 or more just to prepare one form. This type of work is the bread and butter for many corporate lawyers. Why? Because it's so easy and repetitive. Most of the work can be done by their secretaries, yet you'll be charged enormous sums because they know just how important these documents are to you. But now, there is a way for you to

solve your own corporate recordkeeping problems—without a lawyer or their large fees...

Introducing: The Complete Book of Corporate Forms by Ted Nicholas. With this collection of forms, you'll have virtually all the documents you'll ever need right at your fingertips. All you need do is fill in the blanks and insert the completed form in your record book. It's as simple as that to protect your corporate status.

This entire collection of simplified forms (over 118 in all) comes with clear instructions, as well as samples of completed forms.

Ideal for Existing and New Businesses. So you've been incorporated for a while already, and have not been able to keep up with your records? With *The Complete Book of Corporate Forms*, it's never too late to begin. Just complete a few blanks for the things you've already done and you can catch up in no time. It's perfectly legal, and best of all, it works.

Either way, if you suspect your corporate recordkeeping won't pass muster, or you think you're paying your legal counsel too much for routine paper work, don't delay. Order your copy of *The Complete Book of Corporate Forms* now!

Also Available on Computer Diskette—Save $40!

Normally sold separately for $69.95, now you can receive this complete collection of forms on diskette for just $29.95 when you place your order for *The Complete Book of Corporate Forms* today. Just think of the time and money you'll be able to save with these forms available to you at the press of a button! With our diskettes, you can use your word processing software to maximum advantage. Plus, forms are easily tailored to your specific situation:

- mix and match clauses
- generate multiple forms in succession
- alter layout to suit your style
- add or delete words or phrases

Designed to work with the book in hand, save $40 today when you order both the book and diskette as a set. Your total price: $99.90.

Diskettes are protected by warranty. Be sure to include the appropriate catalog number for your computer format when ordering.

SAVE $1.00! FAX Your Credit Card Order 1-312-836-1021. Or Call Toll Free 800-554-4379.

11

124

Figure 6.7 (continued)

IV. The Established Entrepreneur

How To Get the Job You Really Want in Bad Times or Good

If you feel your job security is in jeopardy, if you are out of work now, if you dislike your present job, or if you are seeking a more fulfilling career, here's your opportunity to get the job you *really* want.

Solve the job-hunting mystery for yourself with the help of this remarkable new book. *How To Get a Top Job in Tough Times* by Ted Nicholas and Bethany Waller. With the competition for good jobs now stronger than ever, the time is right for some major new ideas. Find out how this revolutionary job hunting system can work for you, with its practical, step-by-step instructions and advice on resume writing, interview do's and don'ts, successful self-marketing strategies and more.

Catalog #5615-33
Price: $19.95.

Capitalism for Kids

Written by Karl Hess, this book is unlike any other you or your children have read. For the first time, free market economics is presented simply and clearly. Beginning with lessons on capitalism and economics, this unique book offers practical suggestions on how young people can gain a working knowledge of the business world. Informative and fun! For ages 9 and up.

Catalog #5615-34 Hardcover   Price: $12.95

The 100 Best Jobs for the 1990s And Beyond

"Carol Kleiman does not just describe The 100 Best Jobs—she tells you how to get them."
—Thomas R. Horton, Chairman, American Management Association

If you want to get a jump on the hottest growth industries, read this book. Carol Kleiman, one of the nation's foremost authorities on jobs, taps years of research to consider the future workplace. You learn the trends and the training, skills and knowledge you need to carve a career path and steer small company growth through the changes in the coming decade.

There *will be* well-paying and rewarding careers and high growth industries in the years ahead, and the preparation starts *now*.

Part one focuses on:

- The new demographics, the work force and a global economy
- The future workplace
- Fastest growing fields
- The best jobs to train for
- Tips on getting and keeping jobs
- How to change jobs and prepare for the future

Part two looks at the 100 best jobs, divided into 10 major categories. For each of the 100 jobs, a chart details educational and employment requirements, shows 1990 starting salaries, then projects salaries to 2000.

Catalog #5608-70
Price: $19.95

Collect Every Health Insurance Dollar Due with This Claims Kit Organizer

There's a health insurance crisis and it threatens the health, safety, sanity and financial well being of every American.

Every year, more than 100 million people file health claims amounting to billions of dollars. What if there's a problem?

Authors Carolyn & Elliot Shear show you a proven system to collect everything the health insurance industry owes you. This book outlines easy-to-follow, step-by-step plans and checklists to:

- Eliminate confusion over policy benefits
- Speed up claims processing
- Collect underpaid and denied claims
- Settle with doctors and other providers
- Unravel Medicare paperwork

Includes sample claim forms, a diary to track bills, claims, payments and pockets to organize and retain paperwork.

Anyone who needs to file health claims can save money, time and headaches with *The Health Insurance Claims Kit.*

Catalog #1919-02
Price: $19.95

How To Get the Best Deal on Your Life Insurance

With the life insurance industry undergoing a crisis of confidence, it's more important than ever that *you look out for yourself*.

Here's the book—and the approach—to help you do that. It shows you how to:

- Avoid come-ons and find the best policy
- Get the best service
- Use 11 crucial questions to find the best agent and insurer
- Alter coverage when needs change
- Create and follow a personal plan for financial success

There is nothing more important than a reliable, well-informed agent and an insurer with a solid financial foundation. Now you have a trusted guide through the maze, by Terry R. O'Neill, along with practical tips for finding the company, policy and agent that's *right for you!*

Catalog #1919-01
Price: $22.95

SAVE $1.00! FAX Your Credit Card Order 1-312-836-1021. Or Call Toll Free 800-554-4379.

21

Figure 6.7 Sample Successful Brochure (continued)

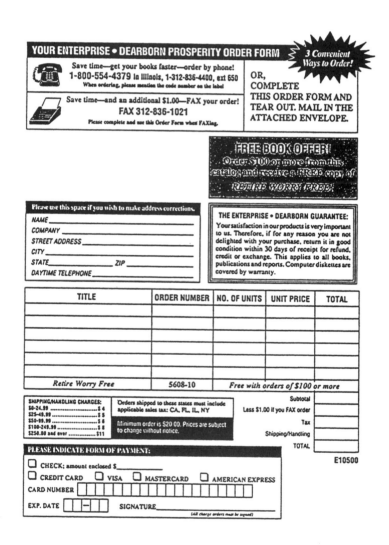

To give you an example of what kinds of information are included in full-page advertisements, and to illustrate the use of the "Eight Basic Truths," we have reprinted one of our successful advertisements in Figure 6.8.

Figure 6.8 Sample Successful Advertisement

The Ultimate Tax Shelter For **ALL** Incomes

by Ted Nicholas

Tax experts are calling a small, privately-owned corporation "the ultimate tax shelter."

Because government has recognized the important role of small business in our country, there are numerous laws favoring corporation owners. With the help of my book, anyone — from any income bracket — can take advantage of this readily available tax shelter.

Anyone Can Incorporate

Small, unincorporated businesses, enjoyable hobbies, part-time businesses, even existing jobs can be set up as full-fledged corporations. I've written HOW TO FORM YOUR OUR CORPORATION WITHOUT A LAWYER FOR UNDER $75, to show you the simplest, fastest and least expensive way to incorporate.

If you're intrigued with the thought of running your own corporation, even on a part-time basis, but don't have a specific idea in mind, I believe my book can stimulate you to action. It's important to remember that you don't need to have a big operation or business to benefit. Ninety-eight percent of businesses in the U.S. are small — often just one person working out of his home.

How You Benefit

Your initial investment can vary from zero to a few hundred or a few thousand dollars. I know it can be done because at age 22, with no capital, credit or experience, I incorporated my first company — a candy manufacturing concern and raised $96,000. From that starting point, grew a chain of 30 stores. You, too, can go as far as your determination and imagination will take you.

When you incorporate, you limit personal liability to your investment in the business. Your home, furniture, and car are not at risk. You can raise capital by borrowing or selling stock and still keep control of your business. You can put

aside up to 25 percent of your income tax free into lucrative retirement, pension, and profit-sharing plans. Your own corporation enables you to maintain continuity and facilitate transfer of ownership. Many tax free fringe benefits can be arranged, such as the deductible health and life insurance programs. Medical and dental expenses for both you and every member of your family can become tax deductible to your corporation. If you wish, you may set up a non-profit corporation or foundation. You can even draw a salary while helping your favorite charity. If you prefer maximum privacy, you may operate anonymously under a pen name you can record for one dollar.

Startling Facts Revealed

Lawyers charge substantial fees for incorporation when often they prefer not to and I'll explain why. You'll discover why two-thirds of the New York and American Stock Exchange companies incorporate in Delaware — the state most friendly to corporations. You'll learn how you can have the same benefits as the largest corporations.

You'll be able to hold all corporate offices: President, Vice-President, and Secretary, if you wish.

What Readers Say

"I was quoted a legal fee of $1,000 each for three corporations I wanted to form. This book saved me almost $3,000!"
— *Joanne Strickland, Wilmington, DE*

"This book succeeds . . . because it fills a real need."
— *PUBLISHER'S WEEKLY*

"Please accept my many thanks for a great book and "Do It Yourself Kit" for the little guy to be able to incorporate without all the hassles and added expenses that normally transpire."
— *John Silvestri, Coral Springs, FL*

Free Bonus

As a bonus for ordering my book, HOW TO FORM YOUR OWN CORPORATION WITHOUT A LAWYER FOR

UNDER $75, I'll send you absolutely free THE INCOME PLAN. This portfolio of valuable information which normally sells for $19.95 shows you how to convert almost any job into your own corporation. You could increase your take-home pay by up to 31 percent without an increase in salary. Employers will also save time and money on payroll records and withholding taxes.

My Personal Guarantee

If you are not completely satisfied with my book, return it undamaged within 30 days, and your money will be promptly refunded. And even if you do return it, THE INCOME PORTFOLIO is yours to keep.

Ted Nicholas

Save $300 to $1500

You'll save from $300 to $1500 simply by using the convenient tear-out forms included in my book. Everything you need is there: certificates of incorporation, minutes, by-laws, and complete instructions.

In a hurry? Orders may be faxed to Nicholas Direct, Inc. 302-529-7567 mail coupon below.

Mail To:
Nicholas Direct, Inc. Dept.
1000 Oakfield Lane,
Wilmington, DE 19810

Please mail ___ copies of HOW TO FORM YOUR OWN CORPORATION WITHOUT A LAWYER FOR UNDER $75 by Ted Nicholas O $19.95 plus a $2.95 postage and handling fee. It is my understanding if I am not completely satisfied with the book, I may return it within 30 days of receipt for a prompt refund and keep the Income Portfolio, normally $19.95, for my trouble.

___ I enclosed my check for $19.95 + $2.95 Shipping & Handling

___ Charge my ☐ Visa ☐ Mastercard ☐ AmEx

_____ exp. date ____

Signature _____
My name is _____
I live at _____
City _____ State ___ Zip Code ____

Fax credit card orders to:
1-302-529-7567

© Nicholas Direct, Inc. 1992

If coupon is missing, send orders to Nicholas Direct, Inc. 1000 Oakfield Lane, Wilmington, DE 19810

Here's an example of how to launch a $100,000-a-year newsletter with **virtually no marketing cost**.

The copy in Figure 6.9 attracted over 1,000 subscribers to a newsletter I conceived by simply writing a letter and enclosing it in a book my company published entitled *The Inside Guide to Complete Asset Protection*. On the outside of the plain envelope these words were typed: "An urgent message from the author. Please open immediately."

Figure 6.9 Newsletter Offer

Would You Invest $97 in a Newsletter if It Helped Protect Your Life Savings and Other Personal Assets while Keeping You Lawsuit and Judgment Proof? What if the Newsletter Came with an Unconditional Guarantee?

This lawsuit and liability explosion we're living in today can ruin you overnight. But now you can protect yourself and your business from judgments, creditors, lenders ... even the IRS.

It's tragic but true. A massive lawsuit . . . nasty divorce . . . business disaster . . . or whopping tax liability can bring instant financial ruin to you and your family. Nothing you own is safe. Your home . . . business . . . savings . . . investments . . . even your paycheck is on the line when trouble strikes. But by then it's too late.

Don't make the mistake of thinking that it could never happen to you. It definitely can. The answer to avoiding disaster is taking some surprisingly simple steps to protect yourself.

There is an urgent need for information on asset protection now. For you, your family and your business.

You've already taken the first step. Your new book, *The Inside Guide to Complete Asset Protection*, will be an invaluable information source for you. But you need the very latest information on a timely basis.

Other lawyers and I are constantly working on new "judgment proofing" and "lawsuit immunity" techniques. As new approaches are developed almost daily, you should know about them.

128

Figure 6.9 (continued)

There is a crucial need for executives, small business owners and their advisors to keep up-to-date. Recent court decisions, as well as new laws and regulations, are constantly changing.

Announcing the *Lawsuit and Asset Protection Letter*

I edit a new monthly newsletter you can't afford to be without. The information in it is indispensable to anyone with assets to protect. It's called the *Lawsuit and Asset Protection Letter*.

Discover easy-to-apply tips and strategies that will help you build and maintain a fortress of protection around all your assets. Written in layperson's language, you'll also receive ready-to-use forms with instructions so you can apply them to your own personal situation. You'll also receive an "Action of the Month" that you can quickly and easily put to use.

The frightening trends and solutions.

There are many new cases which allow the corporate "veil" to be pierced. If so, all your personal assets are put in jeopardy. The *Lawsuit and Asset Protection Letter* will guide you in solving problems such as:

- How to protect yourself personally if you have $1 million in liability coverage and you are sued for $15 million and lose.

- Avoid loss of all your personal assets if your corporation is sued and you are held responsible as an officer or director.

- Prevent creditors from seizing assets in children's and spouse's names for your business obligations.

- Avoid personal bankruptcy if you or your spouse is secretary of a corporation.

- Protect your personal assets when your insurance company becomes insolvent.

- Realistic alternatives to skyrocketing malpractice and liability insurance premiums.

- Avoid malpractice insurance claims after you retire for events which happened years ago.

- When it can be a disaster if property ownership has the designation of joint tenancy, tenancy by the entirety or community property.

- Insulate your assets once a suit has been filed or legal action is pending.

- Prevent creditors from seizing assets held in irrevocable and revocable trusts.

129

Figure 6.9 Newsletter Offer (continued)

- The *Lawsuit and Asset Protection Letter* shows you the latest developments on:
    * maximizing the personal benefits to you of corporations and partnerships.
    * how to control all your investments so you get maximum benefits from them without any liability.
    * how to own real estate without personal liability.
    * how to safely buy distressed property and companies.
    * how to keep creditors happy and supplying you when you need to delay payment.
    * stopping the IRS from seizing assets when you owe them money.
    * settling debts amicably without bankruptcy.
    * what states are the best places to transfer assets.
    * latest developments in prenuptial and cohabitation agreements which give the most protection.
    * using banks and laws of other countries such as Canada, Austria and Switzerland to legally and ethically protect assets.

Who needs this unique newsletter? Business owners, executives, accountants, corporate officers, CPAs, doctors and other professionals, lawyers, bankers, life insurance agents and financial advisors.

You've worked long and hard for your life savings and other personal assets. If you are like most people, your assets are far greater than you realize. When you add up your investments, cash, savings, home, furniture, cars, life insurance, jewelry, etc., the total can quickly rise to $100,000–$250,000 or more. If you own a business, your net worth is probably higher.

We live in a litigation-happy society in which over 750,000 lawyers practice. A single lawsuit can become a costly nightmare. Chances are someone is considering suing you right now! With all of today's legal hazards, doesn't it make sense to keep abreast of the latest news and developments on protecting assets?

Subscribe to the *Lawsuit and Asset Protection Letter* now. Protect your life savings and other personal assets, and learn techniques to help your clients do the same. There is absolutely no risk. The charter subscription price of $97 (normally $147) is tax deductible.

Figure 6.9 (continued)

Money-Back Guarantee

Subscribe to the newsletter without risk of any kind. If you are not completely happy with your subscription after trying it for three months, you will receive a prompt and courteous refund.

To subscribe, call 813-596-4966 now, or complete the subscription request below.

Sincerely,

P.S. If your subscription is received within 30 days, you are guaranteed the special charter rate of $97, and it's fully tax deductible.

- -

YES. Please enter my one-year subscription for the *Lawsuit and Asset Protection Letter* at the special charter rate of $97 (normally $147 a year).

I understand that if it does not live up to my highest expectations, I may cancel anytime within three months and receive a prompt and courteous refund.

[ ] One Year	$ 97	
[ ] Two Years	170	Save $24
[ ] Best Deal—Three Years	240	Save 51

[ ] Enclosed Is My Check

[ ] Charge My   [ ] VISA   [ ] MasterCard   [ ] AmEx

[ ] Diner's Club/Carte Blanche

Name _____

Company Name (if applicable) _____

Address _____

City_____ State _____ Zip _____

Daytime Phone _____

(If we have a question on your order)

Mail to: Nicholas Direct, Inc.
                19918 Gulf Blvd. #7
                Indian Shores, FL 34635

- -

131

Trade Sales

Another avenue open to you is "trade sales." This refers to the bookstore and library markets. To gain maximum exposure, contact commissioned salespeople. This is a sales force independent of any one publisher which travels the country (or a specific territory) and offers all kinds of books for sale.

The Drawbacks

Of course there are disadvantages to this method. The biggest disadvantage of trade selling is a) the length of time it takes to get paid (it can be as long as six months) and b) the problem of consignment selling wherein it's customary that books can be returned.

You also must pay the salesperson a commission on every book sold. However, it's usually well worth it.

The Advantage

The advantage is that your book gets into bookstores and libraries. That's important, and it's worth discounting your retail price in order to gain this exposure. Some book buyers simply will not order a book through the mail. If their bookstore does not stock it, they will have them order it for them or do without it. These people are unusual but must be considered just the same.

When retail stores or libraries order books from you, you will have to give them a discount. The following is a wholesale discount schedule I used for many years at Enterprise Publishing:

Wholesale Discount Schedule

One copy .... No discount
2--4 copies .... 20% discount
5--9 copies .... 30% discount
10--24 copies .... 40% discount
25--49 copies .... 43% discount
50--99 copies .... 46% discount

100 or more copies................ 50% discount

Terms: Net 30 days, F.O.B our shipping point. Publisher reserves the right to require cash with order in establishing new accounts.

Telephone Orders: Any order may be directed to the Order Department, telephone 1-800-554-4379.

Delivery Terms: F.O.B. our warehouse. We will pay shipping and handling costs on all prepaid orders.

Shipping: Our standard shipping procedure is to send books fourth class book rate and ship large quantities by truck. Please specify if you require shipments by other methods.

Return Policy: All returns must be in resaleable condition. No returns before one (1) year from date of invoice.

The Key Contact Function

When selling to bookstores and libraries, I developed a position called "Key Contact." This is a person (undoubtedly you, initially) responsible for contacting all retailers, wholesalers, libraries, schools, reviewers and subsidiary rights buyers. This position completely replaces a commissioned sales force. The majority of contacts are made by phone or through the mail, hence the name.

To begin your own key contact function, it is important to make a list of the major bookstores in the country, the major reviewers and the other publishers who might be most interested in "subsidiary rights." Subsidiary rights refer to book, overseas, reprint, serial, television and motion picture rights.

The names of these people are readily available in *Literary Market Place*, available through R. R. Bowker, 121 Chanlon Road, New Providence, NJ 07974, or through your library. If your subject lends itself to a "talk show" format on radio or television, make a list of these people, too.

Sales prospect names can come from people who have already purchased your book or indicated an interest in it. For instance, if your hometown bookstore proprietor expressed a willingness to take a look at your book when it is published, add this name to your list. If the librarian in your hometown is enthusiastic about recognizing "native talent," be sure his or her name is included. Go through LMP carefully, and make a list of any and all reviewers who might be interested in your book.

Once your list is compiled, plan a campaign of telephone calls and letters. Use the news release techniques (discussed in Chapter 4), and send a copy of the jacket design to the people on the list. Offer to send them a review copy of the book at their request.

Review Copies

In about 30 days, you will receive responses. Get the review copies out immediately to those who requested them. Make a notation of the date the copy was sent next to each name. Go through the list again, and note the people from whom you did not receive a reply to your news release. Take a few minutes to analyze what the reason might be. Does your book seem to "fit" with their reviewing your book, buying copies of your book for their stores or buying subsidiary rights? If the answer is "yes," call them.

Planning Your "Pitch"

Prepare a short "script" of what you plan to say. This always helps, not only in building confidence but also in organizing your thoughts. Separate the reviewers, bookstore buyers and subsidiary rights people. Prepare special scripts for each. Then call them.

Ask if they received your information. If they did not, use this opportunity to tell them a bit about your book, and ask if they might like to see a review copy. If they did receive your release, ask for their reactions. With bookstores, inform them of your discount schedule, and attempt to sell them copies of your book. With reviewers, enumerate the book's strong points once again, and tell them you'll be happy to put a copy in the mail today. With subsidiary rights buyers, be prepared with reasons why your book would be perfect for their readers, viewers, listeners, etc.

Getting Through to the Right Person

Talk to the right person. In publishing companies, personnel switch jobs frequently. Even the newest edition of LMP may not be 100 percent accurate when it comes to names. Ask for the person listed. If they are no longer with that company, ask who might help you. When you get through to someone, outline the nature of your call, and ask if he or she is the person you need to talk to. This one simple question can save a lot of time and money.

Contacting Bookstore Chains

One question often asked deals with the major bookstore chains. Should you call their headquarters to try to arrange a multi-store sale? Yes. After you have sent your news release and other information about your book. Enclose a review copy in this initial package. Follow up with a phone call, make sure you are speaking to the right person responsible for actually buying the books and give it your best shot. When a bookstore chain has outlets all over the country, it can pay to make a personal visit.

Your Prime Contacts

Once reviews of your book have been published and you've made sales to bookstores, keep the names of these reviewers and buyers clearly designated on your list. They are prime contacts and will be the first people to notify when your second book is in the works.

Earlier I covered some key elements of direct response selling. Even though "key contact" is an extremely important function of your publishing venture, I must emphasize again that the most effective method of reaching the most potential book buyers at the lowest cost is direct response. This involves space advertising and direct mail directly to the final customer.

Generating More Sales

Over the course of a year or more, when using direct response methods, the total investment in advertising and promotion if you are intent on building your book into a bestseller may seem sizeable. However, the money will not be put up as advance capital. It will instead flow from pyramiding revenue derived from sales. For example, if you purchase a classified ad for $20 and realize $40 in sales, your gross profit is $20. Part of the $20 profit then goes into more advertising to generate more sales, and so on.

The secret lies in spending advertising dollars only where they generate sales. That's why there is no such thing as an expensive or cheap advertising medium.

If a full-page advertisement in a national men's magazine costs $30,000, but you receive $60,000 as a result of it, that magazine is not expensive. You've made a shrewd advertising buy. On the other hand, if you spend $20 for a third-page ad in the *Podunk Daily Blatt* and receive nothing in sales, you have wasted $20. The measure of success is profit. One good rule of thumb is: "Income must at least double the cost of advertising" for it to be a profitable ad.

Figure 6.10 is a form similar to ones used by many publishing companies to determine the profit and loss of their advertising.

Figure 6.10 Profit and Loss from Advertising Placement

ADVERTISING RESULTS OF _date_

Key No.	Media	Start Date	Page No.	Ad Code	No. Orders	Order Margin	Cost	Total Sales	Gross Margin	Sales Change	Raw Profit or Loss	Cost per \$ Sales
AB-1	AB Magazine	6/2	15	001	251	12.58	1,000	3,752	3,158	598	2,158	.26
CD-1	CD Newspaper	6/6	38	001	41	12.58	205	613	516	30	311	.33
EF-1	EF Newspaper	6/5	64	001	3	12.58	275	45	38	15	(237)	6.11
GH-1	GH Newsletter	6/15	9	001	8	12.58	25	120	101	15	76	.20
IJ-1	IJ Magazine	6/4	126	001	236	12.58	2,463	3,528	2,969	299	606	.69

(handwritten annotations pointing to columns: date you received order; from checking copy; your ad number; number of orders; retail price minus production cost per book (ex. $14.95 retail – $2.37 cost per = 12.58 margin); net cost of ad; number of orders times retail price; number of orders times order margin; dollar amount change since last accounting; gross margin minus cost; cost divided by total sales)

From the previous accounting, which publication would seem to be your best advertising purchase to date? Well, you can look at it in several ways.

The Total Sales Figure

If you were to take the *total sales* figure as the criterion on which to base your decision, publications *AB* and *IJ* would seem to be the most profitable since they had respective total sales of $3,752 and $3,528. But you can't use this figure alone because you will need to deduct what the book cost to produce. This is reflected in the *order margin*. This figure ($12.58 on the chart) is arrived at by taking the retail price of your book ($14.95 in this case) and subtracting the production cost ($2.37) to come up with the profit you make by selling each copy of your book. To arrive at the *gross margin* figure, you multiply the *order margin* ($12.58) by the number of orders. This gives you the *gross margin*, which is the profit you have made from the sales of that many copies of the book.

The Gross Margin

The gross margin alone cannot be considered as a complete picture of your profit either. You must also subtract the money you paid for the advertisement to appear in the magazine. So to arrive at your *raw profit or loss*, you subtract the money you paid for the ad from the gross margin. When comparing the gross margins of publications *AB* and *IJ*, you can see that *AB* made much more money ($2,158) than did *IJ* ($506). The reason is that *IJ* was more than twice as expensive as *AB*.

The *cost per $ sales* figure is another helpful way of putting your profit or loss into black-and-white. This is determined by dividing the *cost* of the advertisement by the *total sales*. This shows you how many dollars or fractions of dollars you have spent for each dollar of sales brought in by that particular ad.

Let's look at *CD Newspaper* and *EF Newspaper*. They have relatively similar costs ($205 and $275), but look at the differences in *cost per $ sales*. This means that you spent $.33 for every dollar of sales on the ad in *CD* and $6.11 on every dollar of sales on the ad in *EF*. Even though you lost only $237 on the ad in *EF* (which was more than offset by the profits on the other ads), you cannot spend $6.11 for each dollar of sales. You could go bankrupt very quickly if you were to spend large sums of money in media that lose money. On the other hand, you must continually seek new markets; so you'll always have some losers, too.

The Cost Per $ Sales

The cost per $ sales in *GH Newsletter* is the lowest figure among all of your ads ($.20). But if you look carefully, this one is not a very profitable ad for you. You have sold only eight books. You are not going to generate volume sales this way.

Clearly, the ad in *AB Magazine* is your best buy.

Sales Change

Now, what about the *sales change* column of figures? This means the dollar amount of change since the last accounting. A sales change of $598 means that you have sold 40 books since the last time you worked out the figures ($598 divided by $14.95). A sales change of $15 means that only one book was sold.*

Start Date

Start date is the day you receive the first order. You can expect your ad's sales change to be high soon after publication, then it will peak and gradually taper off to nothing. In a magazine published monthly, if your ad has just "broken" (you just started to receive orders), your sales change will be higher than an ad that has been pulling orders for several weeks and has already peaked. If you look at the chart again, and notice the sales changes and start dates on publications *EF* and *GH*, you will again see something interesting.

EF has been pulling for 10 days longer than *GH*, yet it has only three orders, whereas *GH* has eight. Chances are very good that *GH* will continue to pull orders for a few more weeks, making the ad even more profitable than it is at this point.

Position

Another thing to consider is the *position* of your advertisement. On what *page* does it appear in the publication? This can strongly affect the pulling power of your ad. Notice the page positions of *AB* and *IJ*. Perhaps one of the reasons why *IJ* is not doing so well

---

*Figures are rounded to the nearest dollar.

is that it is positioned toward the back of the magazine. *AB* is close to the front. It makes you wonder what the ad in *IJ* would have done if it had been on page 15 like the ad in *AB*.

Experience has taught me that the closer your ad is to the front of the magazine, the more orders you get.

Key Numbers

The *key number* is of vital importance. An ad without a key number will be almost worthless. (This is in terms of tracking information and response rates.) You must know specifically which publication your order comes from. Without a method of determining which publications work best, you are throwing money away.

The most common way of deciding on a key number is to make it easily identifiable.

You will note that "AB-1" is the key number that appeared on the ad in *AB Magazine*. The "1" relates to the first ad you have placed in that magazine, or it could relate to the month in which it appeared. My own company's system of keying advertisements is to give the initials of the magazines, the year it appeared, the month and the book code.

For instance the key number "PD-29C" would relate to *Physician's Digest* in 1992, in the 9th month, and the ad was for the "Corporation Book."

If we ran two ads in the same month in the same publication for two different books (let's say the Corporation and Self-publishing books), the key numbers would be "PD-29C" and "PD-29S."

When keying ads, place the key number in the address next to the word "Dept." For example,

Nicholas Direct, Inc.
1000 Oakfield Lane, Dept. PD-29C
Wilmington, DE 19810

would be the way in which the key number would appear in the return address in the advertisement.

The Best Lists

Generally, stick with lists of people who are accustomed to buying products through the mail. Even if a targeted group of people seem to be prime targets for your direct mail campaign, if they have not bought through the mail before, the test will be risky. Reason? Some people just don't like to order things through the mail.

When you make offers to people who have never bought anything by mail, they have a built-in resistance to your offer from the start.

Mail order buyers, however, like the convenience of ordering through the mail and are accustomed to the process involved. Mail order buyers also understand that it sometimes takes up to 30 days to receive the product, and they are more willing to be patient.

If you are faced with a choice between two lists that are identical in all respects except that one is made up of recognized mail-order buyers, go with it.

Analyzing a Mailing List

To analyze the potential of any list you are considering, review these points:

- **How often the people on the list have ordered products through the mail.** This is an important consideration. Go with the list of buyers who purchase often and regularly rather than just once.
- **How up-to-date is the list?** Get the most recent list available, such as those who have purchased within the last 90 days.
- **How much money was involved in the purchase?** Choose lists where the retail price plus postage and handling matches

or is greater than the product you are selling. A list of people who sent $1 for six packets of seeds may not be the same people who will send $14.95 for a book on gardening.

- **How the people paid for the product ordered.** If a list is composed of mainly credit card buyers and you are not offering that option, you might not have as much success as you would with a list that paid by check.

- **Is the list comprised of buyers, or are they inquirers?** Although inquiries can sometimes be hot prospects, stick with the people who actually bought the product after inquiring about it.

- **Is the product bought similar to or competitive with yours?** A list of people who have bought a book on the same general topic can be profitable.

- **Check for seasonal elements in the list you are considering.** Millions of people buy through the mail at Christmas, but will the same people buy your book in June?

- **Review the demographics.** If it is important that potential buyers of your book be male homeowners with a college education, demographics are of vital importance. Included in the list information package will be a breakdown of the buyer's age, sex, marital status, family composition, family income, home ownership, location, education, etc.

Keep these considerations in mind when analyzing lists for your direct mail.

Another big element is the cost of renting the list. What will it cost you to do the mailing? How many books will you have to sell before you break even and start realizing a profit?

How To Determine Mailing Costs

A simple way of figuring this out on paper is to use a chart shown in the example below. As in space advertising, you will need to key all response devices so that you can track your results and chart the effectiveness of each list and each mailing piece. Knowing your exact costs will also be essential in determining the profitability of each mailing.

List Name:_____ Offer: _____

List Source: _____ Qty Mailed: ___Date Mailed: _____

Production Cost: _____

Inserting/Mailing Cost: _____

List Rental Cost:_____

Postage Cost: _____

Total Net Cost: _____

Once these costs are established, profitability is calculated in exactly the same manner as were space ads, illustrated earlier in this chapter.

Determining the suitability of mailing lists is also the same as deciding which magazines will be best for space ads.

Orders with No Traceable Source

There are always orders coming in that cannot be traced to their sources. These are inevitable and due to many reasons, such as that your customer simply sent a letter and check for your book and omitted the source code. The reasons for orders arriving without key numbers are varied. Another reason is that the customer did not want to deface the magazine by cutting out the coupon. Or he or she simply addressed the envelope and left out the department number. Other reasons have to do with "word-of-mouth": The customer heard about your book from some source other than your advertisement. While it can be somewhat annoying to receive unkeyed orders, I've always welcomed these orders and treated them as unexpected bonus orders!

On your chart, simply add a line called *No Source* to keep track of the number of orders.

Chapter 7

How To Get the Best Advertising Buys

You always have the option of finding an advertising agency to help you with the problem of getting your message out. But I don't recommend this approach. I review in the next chapter how to start your own small house agency.

You can get better rates on space and direct mail lists than any agency can in most cases. I also feel that the person who writes the book is also the best person to write selling copy for it. If you wrote your book, you know what's in it and why it is a benefit to other people.

Analyzing a List or Magazine

As discussed previously, direct mail is one of the most cost-effective ways to get your book to your customers. It is selective. Your sales pitch goes only to those people who would be interested in buying your book. You can choose from thousands of lists of names. These are broken down into specific categories, which include age, income level, interest in particular subjects, frequency of purchases by mail, sex, geographical location, when each placed his or her last order for merchandise and the amount of money spent ordering

145

products through the mail. These categories are referred to as the "demographics."

Where To Go for Help

There is an excellent organization that can be very helpful: Direct Marketing Association, Inc., 11 West 42nd Street, New York, NY 10036-8096. Write for a list of their publications.

The Circulation Figures

When you analyze a magazine for space advertising, take the demographics into consideration as well as the audited circulation. Is the circulation guaranteed, or has the publisher stated the figures in "pass-along" readership? When someone reads a magazine and then gives it to a friend, this is considered "pass-along." This can be valuable in boosting your exposure to the greatest number of people, but pass-along readership is never guaranteed. It is frequently only an estimate of the publisher's marketing department, so be wary of it.

Repeat Advertisers

Look through the magazine carefully. How much mail order advertising appears in it? Read several back issues. Determine which advertisers repeat their ads month after month. This is a good sign that tells you they were successful in that publication. If they are offering a product that is in the same general category as yours, you can be assured that the magazine readers are book buyers. Otherwise the company wouldn't continue to run their ads in the magazine.

The Magazine's Editorial Slant

Read the articles. Magazine publishers are acutely aware of the values and interests of their readers. You can get a good idea of what the readers are like by the nature, tone, depth and scope of the articles. For example, if your book is a light-hearted pop psychology self-improvement book, it might not go over too well in a serious scientific publication. Use your intuition. Try to imagine what the readers are like and whether they would be interested in buying your book.

Requesting Information

When you request information from the magazine, indicate that you might be interested in advertising in it. They will send you a *media kit* consisting of a rate card, sample issue and a demographic printout. Review this information thoroughly before making your decision. Always ask for special discounts for publishers and mail order merchandisers. Ask for the very best *test rate* they can offer you. Many publications offer these discounts. Seldom do they appear on the rate cards.

Locating the people who are most interested in your subject is the secret of successful mail order selling. Although magazines offer a less-selective audience than direct mail, you can find publications that cater to the needs of people who are interested in your subject. New magazines are being born almost every day in this country, and many are designed for highly specialized audiences. If you are diligent in your search, you will probably find a magazine that is a perennial winner for you, where you can advertise over and over again at a profit.

Rate Protection

If you find a proven magazine in which you can run your ads frequently, negotiate further with the publisher. Ask for rate protection. You will agree to place so many ads per year. In return, they agree to guarantee you a low rate. Be more demanding in your position requests. If your results show that your ad does better on a right-hand page, as is usual, tell the publisher that you must have a right-hand page. You are important to the magazine. Remember that subscriptions do not pay for magazines; the advertisers do.

How To Get Free Advertising and Publicity

Even free advertising is wasted if it fails to generate sales. It is rare, however, when advertising fails to stimulate some sales with proven ad copy.

By itself, free or no-risk advertising will not provide enough promotional "muscle" to create a bestseller. It *can* be used in conjunction with paid advertising to provide better coverage.

You can also test the effectiveness of a medium about which you are in doubt. In this way you shift the risk from yourself to the publication.

I will now reveal to you the safest and most profitable advertising method!

The "P. O." Ad

A prime method of advertising with no risk on your part is what is referred to as a "P.O." These initials stand for *per order*. This means that the newspaper, magazine, radio or television station runs your advertisement without cost to you. When the orders come in, the publication or station takes their cut (usually a 33 to 50 percent commission) of the retail selling price. They then send the balance to you along with the orders. You share the profit. There is no risk to you whatsoever.

You would not want to enter a P.O. arrangement with a medium you have tested with good results. In that case, why split the profits? Instead, pay for the advertising, and collect all the revenue.

Let's say that you have selected a magazine that fits your needs. (Analyses of particular magazines will be demonstrated later.) This magazine's rates seem to be beyond your means especially since you have never run an ad in it. Their full-page rate is $6,000. You know that you will need to sell approximately 1,200 copies of your book at $14.95 to make a good profit from the ad ($6,000 divided by 1,200 = $5 cost per order), but you are not sure that the circulation will produce that many orders. The ideal way to go about it is to negotiate for a P.O. When you communicate with the advertising manager, include figures that will make the arrangement attractive. For instance, on the $6,000 ad, if you receive 800 orders, the publication will get their page rate ($6,000) when you offer them a 50 percent commission.

Mathematically, it works out like this:

50% of $14.95 = $7.48
$6,000 divided by $7.48 = 800

So, 800 orders will net the publication their $6,000, and you will have paid nothing. So YOU made $6,000 total sales on the arrangement as well (800 x $14.95 = $11,960 total sales).

Once you have established that you can indeed pull enough orders from a full-page advertisement in this publication, you can run an ad again and again. More publications are receptive to this arrangement than you might think, so don't hesitate to ask for it.

You can also do "P.I." ads, which stands for *per inquiry*. In this circumstance you arrange to pay for each person (or lead) who inquires for more information about the product. Payment for P.I.'s can be from 50 cents to $5 or more. A typical inquiry payment for a $40 to $80 book, newsletter or tape is about $2.

How To Approach Radio and TV Stations

The best way to approach busy television and radio talk show hosts is through a short, personal letter (or even a postcard on colored stock) stating three or four of the most interesting benefits of your material and a biography of the author. Such a letter ought to be written, or at least signed, by someone other than yourself. Television people particularly are accustomed to dealing through a third party. And sometimes it's easier for someone else to extol your virtues in print.

Mentioning the Key Points

In deciding which points to cover about the book, draw upon the same ones you used in making up your advertisement. Exactly the same benefits that must be used to sell your book to consumers must be used with TV and radio producers.

Capturing Attention

One good way to capture the television host's or producer's attention is to relate the subject of your book to a topical problem of the day. For example,

> "Mr. Doe's book, *Secrets of Organic Gardening*, helps provide answers to today's shrinking food dollar."

Then reveal a few of those secrets in the letter.

The important thing to remember is that television and radio people are constantly looking for fresh material to present to their viewers or listeners. Most talk shows are broadcast five days a week, and even a 5- or 10-minute show runs through a lot of material in a month's time. The hosts and producers look for authors as a prime source of material.

Don't ignore local shows. People love to see a local author. It raises their pride in their town or city and gives them something to talk about. Don't forget to mention that you are a past resident if this is the case. Just the fact that you once lived in an area can be enough to get you air time on a talk show.

One way to get national exposure for your book without travel time or expense is through radio call-in shows. You can do them from your home or office. They can be a source of volume sales of your book as well as lots of fun.

Recently, in a single day, I did 22 consecutive radio shows all across America. The audience was over eight million listeners. And book sales were outstanding! Over 600 radio stations across the country do telephone interviews. And you don't have to leave your office with all the attendant time and travel expense involved!

Interview with the Author

Usually when you are asked to be a guest on a road tour, you will go through a screening process. The interviewer will sit down with you and chat for a few minutes about your book. Sometimes a video tape will be made of this informal discussion, in the case of television, so that producers and technicians can see how you come across on camera. Be natural and be yourself. Try to avoid nervous gestures such as squirming in your chair. Don't answer with simple "yes" or "no" responses. Sound enthusiastic about your book. Get other people excited enough about it to buy it from you!

In your letter to the station you will want to close with a request for an appointment and a specific date for the broadcast of your appearance. It helps to offer a time frame of two weeks or so for the host to work within. With the first letter you can simply enclose a sales circular for your book. When you go in for the appointment, the host will undoubtedly request a copy of your book.

Preparation for the Show

Sometimes the host will have read or skimmed your book before your appearance, sometimes not. Almost always, someone at the station will have at least skimmed it. Prepare a list of questions for the host to ask you. Be prepared for just about anything. If the host has not read your book, you will need to do more talking to get across the major points.

Through this method, my company has booked appearances for our authors, including myself, on hundreds of radio and television shows throughout the country. Figure 7.1 is a sample letter.

Figure 7.1 Sample Letter to Radio/Television Show Host

Dear Producer/Interviewer:

Have you ever dreamed of being your own boss—perhaps owning your own corporation?

Just about all of us have at one time, but many of us are afraid to take a chance. The American dream seems just that—a dream.

SO WHAT'S STOPPING US?

Many people are put off as much by the perceived complicated red tape and legal expense as by the fear of failure or losing money.

Business expert and entrepreneur Ted Nicholas can help. This founder of over 22 diverse corporations has helped to inspire people throughout the world to start and succeed in their own business.

In his book, *How To Form Your Own Corporation Without a Lawyer for under $75* (Enterprise • Dearborn, $19.95), Nicholas has devised a system of self-incorporating that allows entrepreneurs to avoid the legal fees and confusion of incorporation. With over 900,000 copies in print, this bestselling, step-by-step guide, now in its 20th anniversary edition, has helped thousands learn how quick, easy and inexpensive the process can be.

In clear, concise language, the book:

- Offers advice on which type of corporation works best for you in your state.

- Provides step-by-step instructions on how to set up a corporation without a lawyer at minimal cost (including the legal forms).

- Outlines the many advantages and benefits to incorporating (such as tax deductions, insurance rates and capital raising).

Ted Nicholas can share a proven, successful method for success with your audience members and readers who are ready to go for it and reap the benefits of their hard work—personally!

I'll be in touch with you soon to see if we can arrange an interview.

Cordially,   **L.A./San Diego, 5/22-26**   **Philadelphia, 6/8**

                 New York, 6/2-3   **Washington, D.C. 6/9-10**

                 Boston, 6/4-5   **Atlanta, 6/12**

How To Promote Your Book Through Magazine Articles

An excellent means of obtaining free publicity is to offer to write articles for a magazine or newspaper. To engineer such a deal, write to the editor of the magazine. Mention that you are willing to write an article for the magazine at no cost, slanted toward the magazine's audience. Request a mention about your book at the end of the article that includes where readers can buy it. Large volume book sales can often result. And they are very profitable because there is no advertising cost. The only thing invested is your time.

Why This Promotion Is Likely To Work

Two things are in your favor in such an arrangement. First, as the author, you are an authority on the subject. Magazines want authorities writing articles for them. Second, most publications are on tight budgets, and the mention of a "freebie" makes an editor's heart warm. When you contact the editor, it would be helpful to have an outline of your article. Make sure that you have studied the magazine to see what type of articles it generally runs.

Magazines of all types and sizes run articles in this way, and I've had many published. They are an excellent means of gaining exposure for both yourself and your book.

If you don't feel comfortable with this approach, some writers use another route. You write the article under a pen name. Or have someone else write it for you, and submit it to the magazine under his or her name. An article about you from another party can sell books. If the story is "news" and it is written in a way that appeals to the readership of the magazine, you shouldn't have any problems getting it published especially if you offer it to them free of charge.

Testimonials

Testimonials are an effective method of free promotion. Everyone is interested in the comments and reactions of other people. Your book gains credibility and more sales.

You can get testimonials early in the lifecycle of your book. Perhaps while the book is still in the manuscript stage, show it to business contacts, celebrities, friends, neighbors, coworkers, relatives and others to read and comment on. If you use their names and remarks in subsequent advertising and promotion, get their permission in the form of a written release. Most people won't mind and are usually quite flattered when asked.

Figure 7.2 is a sample testimonial release that we currently use. You can model yours after this.

Figure 7.2 Sample Testimonial Release

Release

I hereby give Nicholas Direct, Inc. the nonrevocable right to use the following comments or portions thereof for the advertising of their products or services.

_____   _____

Signature   Date

_____

Name Typed or Printed as It Should Appear with Testimonial

    Yes _____   No _____

I also give permission to use a photograph of myself, and/or any filmed testimonial should one already exist or be taped in the future.

_____

Signature

By obtaining testimonials early in the promotional effort, you can incorporate them in your title-testing circular, the book jacket, the cover itself (if paperback) and all of your advertising.

The Autograph Party

Still another little- or no-cost method of promoting your book is through conducting an autograph party in one or more bookstores. Many books, of course, lend themselves to this kind of personal touch in promotion.

The procedure is easier than you might think. Start by contacting bookstores in your locale. You can call or drop them a line indicating your availability for an autograph party. The bookstore can promote this in the local newspaper and hopefully attract additional customers to the store to purchase a book signed by you.

Later, if and when you go on a regional or national tour of radio and TV shows, it is a good idea to tie in with bookstores in the areas in which you will appear. You can contact these stores in advance of your appearances on these shows.

Take plenty of books with you to the autograph party. Usually the bookstore will buy the copies and sell them (you give them a 40 percent discount off the retail price depending on quantity).

Autograph parties on my books have ranged from very successful (with people waiting in line to purchase copies) to events when just a few people drop in. A lot depends on your publicity efforts.

Bookstores are usually happy to set up an autograph party because, if handled correctly, it brings more people into the store. If they can coordinate the autographing session with a special event or sale, so much the better. In this way the bookstore and you will be doing each other a favor. Make it an equal trade, and cooperate with them as much as possible. Often, even if a large volume of book sales does not materialize, local publicity of this type helps make your mail order advertising more effective since your exposure is greater.

Newspaper Columnists and Book Reviewers

Reviews get sales. Sometimes even reviews that pan your book tend to arouse reader curiosity about it. The rule here is: Try to get your book reviewed in print as often as you can. But don't waste copies of the book sending it to people who are unlikely to write a review. How do you determine in which category a potential reviewer belongs?

Begin with *Literary Market Place* (LMP). Divide columnists and reviewers into two groups----those likely to write a review and those you're not too sure about. Remember that reviewers are more motivated by the actual book than talk show hosts are. Television people tend to be more interested in you as a personality than in your book. As an expert in your field, you will have a pretty good idea of whom to send the book to for the most likely reviews. For the second group, select those names from your list of reviewers. Send a cover letter offering a review copy of the book if they would be interested in receiving it.

Syndicated Reviewers

If there are syndicated reviewers well known in your field, send a copy of the book on the first shot with a cover letter.

Then determine other potential reviewers. Consult *Ayers Periodical Directory*, *Bacon's Publicity Checker* (all publications are listed by industrial classification) and LMP. Don't overlook the value of a review in your local paper or on the area's radio stations. In fact, in a smaller city, a story about a local author can be Page One news.

When you send review copies or letters of inquiry, follow these up with a phone call or letter. Inquire as to whether the right person received the book and if a review is planned. Sometimes the book never arrives or is routed to the wrong person. If the person you speak with is hesitant to confirm a future review, add a bit more of a sales pitch to the conversation.

Writing Your Own Review

You can obtain additional publicity mileage by writing your own review and getting it printed in newspaper facsimile style. These "clips" can then be mailed to other papers. They are effective in generating more publicity. Sometimes you can use the news release format and presentation for a book review. Simply state at the bottom of the page:

> "This book review may be used in its entirety,
> or in an edited version, without further permis-
> sion clearance."

Often, when you can save an editor time, they will thank you for it by printing your review.

"P.I." on TV and Radio

In addition to appearing on talk shows, you can explore "PI" (per inquiry) arrangements on both radio and TV. You pay the cost of preparing the advertisement. You can contact a local TV station or studio and ask them to prepare a video tape for you. If you have a theatrical flare, you can save yourself about $100 to $200 that you would pay a professional announcer. Since your product is your own book or one you are publishing, you do not need to have a polished announcer advertise it on a TV spot. Your credibility can go a long way toward offsetting your inexperience in front of a camera or microphone.

The cost of producing a one-minute spot will be as low as $500 in a small studio up to several thousand dollars, with an additional $35 to $50 for each duplicate tape. Be sure to get a price in advance.

Rather than sending a tape to a TV station, first send a cover letter and a sales brochure describing the book.

In the letter, ask if they do PI advertising and if they would be interested in running yours. Since PI advertising represents some risk for the station, it will select the product most likely to draw responses. Thus, a good track record of sales makes acceptance easier.

Figure 7.3 is a sample of a first approach letter to make PI arrangements.

Figure 7.3 Sample First Approach Letter

Dear (Station Manager):

Please call me collect at _____. Why?

Because I have something that is going to make both of us a lot of money! What is it? Our publication by Ted Nicholas, *How To Form Your Own Corporation Without a Lawyer for under $75.*

This book is the hottest how-to book on the market today with sales of over 1 million copies. A reader can use the tear-out forms, incorporate and save hundreds of dollars! A lot of idle bragging? Not in the least. This concept has been tested by readers in the United States, Canada, Europe and Mexico, by both amateurs and professionals. It's a proven system. It works.

We're so sure of the sales success of this book that we're putting our money where our mouth is. We're offering this book for only $19.95 postpaid. The buyer can keep the book for 10 days. If he or she is not completely satisfied, we'll refund the money. Fair enough?

What all this means to you is profit, because you keep $8 for every order you receive. I'd be happy to send you our prerecorded (60-second) commercial and a sample book for you to read. Call immediately, and let's both start sharing the profits!

Sincerely,

Enc. (brochure)

P.S. On my shows dozens of copies have already been sold with this proven commercial. And your station receives $8 on every copy. Call me now at _____.

Special Ways To Sell Your Book

Bookstores

While mail order offers the best potential sales for your book, don't overlook the 15,000 book dealers and numerous wholesalers in the United States.

Literary Market Place can put you in touch with dozens of wholesalers. The *American Book Trade Directory* tells who to contact and outlines particular interests of every bookstore and wholesaler in the U. S. and Canada.

As a general rule, bookstores and libraries tend to make purchases through wholesale book distributors. Wholesalers who can merchandise your book through retail shops are found in LMP. Send the wholesaler a letter describing your book and ask him or her to call you and/or send a purchase order.

You also can contact bookstores and department stores directly. One approach is to load up the trunk of your car, and simply start driving. If you call for an appointment, it is easier to be put off by a secretary. If you show up, book in hand, ready to do business, you are bound to make more sales.

Usually, bookstore owners and operators are down-to-earth people who enjoy being exposed to new books. The standard discount was mentioned previously, but you can work your own deals from there, depending on how badly you want the exposure in any particular bookstore or department store.

Don't avoid the large department stores because you assume the managers aren't interested. These establishments sell a large number of books, and their book department managers frequently have more time to sit and discuss your book than do small shop owners who have multiple duties. Also, large department stores have correspondingly large budgets and can afford to gamble more on an unknown author or book.

You will have to work harder than sales representatives from well-known large publishers. But your personal effort and enthusiasm, coupled with your knowledge of your own work, can give you an edge.

A salesperson selling many titles simply can't devote the attention to each one that you can provide for your book. Sales representatives have catalogs full of titles. It really doesn't matter to them which books get sold, only that *some* are purchased by the store. So, unlike you, they will not make a strong effort to sell any one title.

Schools

Schools represent a massive market. Currently 2 million teachers select not only textbooks but also related source materials.

Computerized lists have made possible the fine-tuning of teachers' names and their specific subject areas to which your book might apply. One source of such a list is *Educational Directory*, 126 Blaine Avenue, Marion OH 43302. This firm's strength is its breakdown of college professors into very specific subject categories. Also inquire of: R. R. Bowker, 121 Chanlon Road, New Providence NJ 07974 for their mailing lists to schools.

Other Stores and Special Approaches

Depending on your title, other retailers can sell your book. Approach discount stores, office supply stores, flower shops, greenhouses, health food stores, hardware stores and lawn and garden supply stores. These are all potential and logical places to purchase such a book.

Once you begin marketing your book, all sorts of other possibilities will become obvious to you. Church groups, garden clubs, etc. always need speakers, and what better opportunity to offer autographed copies of your book? County fairs, farmers' markets, gardening sales conventions and trade shows all offer splendid opportunities for setting up a small booth.

The contacts you make at events like these can even be more important than the number of books you sell. Remember that word-of-mouth is sometimes the best, and certainly the cheapest, method of advertising.

In summary, there are many diverse ways to sell your book. Use your imagination. Because every book is unique, you will undoubtedly be able to dream up other ways to sell your book in addition to those I've already mentioned. Try this exercise:

Other Opportunities To Sell Your Book

Where else can you sell your book? Here's where to let your imagination work for you. As you come across more opportunities, write them down as soon as possible. Don't worry if an idea seems farfetched at first. You can always revise or discard it. Your goal is to keep your eyes and ears open for more ways to sell your book. Jot down a few here:

1. _____
2. _____
3. _____
4. _____
5. _____
6. _____
7. _____
8. _____

Chapter 8

You as Publisher: What's Next?

Perhaps the most important aspect of a publishing venture is to approach the merchandising of a book as you would any other product. If you were to embark upon selling cars, for example, you would not begin without a predesigned format for conducting business. You would need a system of keeping records, recording cash transactions, raising operating capital, contacting potential customers and other procedures.

The need for structure is no less critical in merchandising and developing high volume sales for a book.

The Business Venture

Whether you are self-publishing your own book or someone else's, approaching publishing as a business venture offers several advantages. It forces you to think in terms of profit and loss at an early stage. That fact will cause you to make decisions differently than if you were thinking of the manuscript as nothing more than an artistic entity. Also, creating a business structure forces you to keep records. This will be a structure you will be thankful for at

162

income tax time since many of your business-related expenses are deductible from your gross income.

Finally, creating a business makes you examine your assets and liabilities as a publisher. What do you have to offer? What are the strengths and weaknesses of your product? How can you develop your "game plan"?

The Best Bet----A Publishing Company

The most logical type of business for you to create is a publishing company. You will receive all the benefits of building your own business in addition to some others. You can publish your own books or the works of other authors. As you gain experience going through the steps of creating a bestseller, you will see opportunities with other books.

Forming a publishing business also offers you the satisfaction that comes from making your influence felt in the world. As a creator and marketer of information, you will enjoy the prestige and status unknown to other people. The title of "John Doe, Publisher," carries with it a degree of prestige. That fact alone might help you obtain capital if you need to.

Starting Your Own Advertising Agency

While discussing the formation of your business venture, I want to point out the advantages of starting your own advertising agency. Agencies receive a 15 percent discount each time an ad is placed. The publication bills the agency for the total amount less their 15 percent commission. If you are your own advertising agency, you keep that 15 percent commission!

Also, you will be your own best copywriter in most cases. You will undoubtedly work harder than any agency you might hire would work to promote your book. You will also pursue specials and "deals" which provide many opportunities to buy ads at the lowest cost.

Getting 15% Off All Advertising

To start your own agency, select a name different from your publishing company. Get some stationery printed. Incorporate the business separately. You will then get a 15 percent discount from most newspapers and magazines.

A simpler way to place your own ads is to have your publishing company name sound like an ad agency. That is one of the reasons my current company is Nicholas Direct.

The Insertion Order

Figure 8.1 is an example of a typical "insertion order" that your advertising agency would send to magazines and newspapers when you wish to place an ad. You can have these printed attractively. Or simply type the information on your letterhead. In any case, make sure that you find the current rate for the size ad you are placing and the correct address, and provide all of the information contained in the sample insertion order.

Make the insertion order contingent upon the rate and position you specify. In this way, if there is a rate increase of which you are not aware, or if the publication cannot give you the position you request, you will be informed before they run the ad. If they go ahead and run the ad, then bill you at a higher rate, you can point to your insertion order and say, "The order was contingent upon that rate." If they run the ad in a position different from the one specified, chances are good that the publication will give you what is called a "make-good." They will run the ad again in the specified position, usually free of charge, or at a great discount.

Figure 8.1 Typical Insertion Order

ENTERPRISE ADVERTISING, INC.
725 North Market Street
Wilmington, DE 19801
Phone: 1-800-533-2665 Fax: 1-302-654-0277

INSERTION ORDER

*Insertion
Order Number*

SO-365

*Space Contract
Insertion Order*

Date 1/15/92

To: World Beater Magazine

Address: 4895 Olympic Blvd.
Los Angeles, CA 90074

Please Publish the Advertising Of: Nicholas Direct, Inc.

For: World Beater Magazine

Dates of Insertion / Issue	Space Size	Color
March issue	7 x 10	B&W

Position	Ad Code	Key No.
Page 3, 5, 7 or OMIT	G-0037	GWB23

Headline
Incorporate Yourself and Become Judgment Proof

Instructions:

Special Instructions:

☒ Send tear sheet to agency
☒ Send publication to agency
☒ Send tear sheet to client
☒ Return artwork to agency
☐ Hold artwork or plates
☐ Re-run of previous ad
☐ Other _____

Enclosures:

☒ Velox or stat
☐ Negative
☐ Artwork
☐ Artwork to follow
☐ Glossy
☐ Plate or cut
☐ Rough layout
☐ Other _____

Gross Rate _____ 10,000.00
Less Discounts _____ 8,000.00
_____
Net Amount _____ 2,000.00
Less 15% Comm. _____ 300.00
Net Cost _____ 1,700.00
Other _____

Notes: Order is Contingent Upon Rate and Position

Ted Nicholas
Authorized Signature

Per: _____ Ted Nicholas, President

CC: _____

*The Man Who Doesn't Advertise Is Like the Man Who Winks in the Dark . . .
He Knows What He Is Doing But Nobody Else Does*

Media Copy, Accounting, Review, File, Records

© Enterprise Publishing, Inc. 1990

165

Hiring an Advertising Agency

Instead of setting up your own agency, you can hire an advertising agency. At least in theory. However, because there are so few direct marketing–oriented agencies, and of those, fewer still who want to take on a small publisher as a client, I don't recommend this direction.

What Form for Your Business?

Your business can take three basic forms: proprietorship, partnership and corporation. Each has advantages and disadvantages which you can weigh in terms of your own goals. Many individuals have heretofore been deterred from incorporating a business because of the high initial cost and the fact that they did not know how to go about it. For those reasons, I published my first book, mentioned earlier, *How To Form Your Own Corporation Without a Lawyer for under $75*. It contains the tear-out forms for everything you need, including minutes, by-laws and the actual Certificate of Incorporation.

Here are some excerpts from the book outlining the advantages and disadvantages of each form of business:

Advantages of Partnerships and Proprietorships

1. Somewhat lower cost to organize since there are no incorporating fees.
2. Less formality in recordkeeping.
3. The owners file only one tax return.
4. Owners can deduct losses that might be incurred during the early life of a business from other personal income.
5. "Keogh" plans reduce the tax advantage available to corporations for retirement purposes.

166

6. Profits of a partnership, unlike dividends paid by corporations, are not subject to a second federal income tax when distributed to the owners. However, whether this is an advantage, tax-wise, depends on other factors, namely:
   a. The individual tax brackets of the owners as compared with that of the corporation.
   b. The extent to which double taxation of earnings of the corporation is eliminated by deductible salaries paid to owners and by retention of earnings in surplus.

Disadvantages of Partnerships and Proprietorships

1. Unlimited personal liability. The owners are personally liable for all debts and judgments against the business, including liability in case of failure or other disaster.
2. In a partnership, each member can bind the other so that one partner can cause the other to be personally liable.
3. All profits are personally taxable to the owners at rates that may be higher than corporate rates.
4. There aren't the tax advantages of benefit plans such as pension and profit-sharing that are available to corporations. (The "Keogh" type plans for unincorporated businesses that do permit pension and profit-sharing plans do not have the flexibility and tax shelters contained in corporate plans. There is a limit, or ceiling, of $30,000 that any one principal owner or partner can contribute toward a profit-sharing plan.)
5. If the owner(s) dies or becomes incapacitated, the business often comes to a standstill.
6. The owner(s) does not have the full tax benefits of the tax-deductible plans including pension and profit-sharing that are available to a corporation.

167

Advantages of Incorporating

1. The personal liability to the founders is limited to the amount of money put into the corporation with the exception of unpaid taxes.

2. If a business owner wishes to raise capital, a corporation is more attractive to investors who can purchase shares of stock in it for purposes of raising capital.

3. A corporation does not pay tax on monies it receives in exchange for its own stock.

4. Many more tax options are available to corporations than to proprietorships or partnerships. One can set up pension, profit-sharing and stock option plans that are favorable to the owner of the corporation.

5. A corporation can be continued more easily in the event of the death of its owners or principals.

6. Shares of a corporation can easily be distributed to family members.

7. The owners (shareholders) of a corporation that is discontinued due to its being unsuccessful can have all the advantages of being incorporated, yet be able to deduct from personal income up to $50,000 on an individual tax return, or $100,000 on a joint return of money invested in the corporation.

8. The owners (shareholders) of a corporation can operate with all the advantages of a corporation, yet be taxed on personal income tax rates if this option provides a tax advantage.

9. Owners can quickly transfer their ownership interest represented by shares of stock without the corporation dissolving.

10. The corporation's capital can be expanded by issuing and selling additional shares of stock.

11. Shares of stock can be used for estate and family trust planning.

12. The corporation can ease the tax burden of its shareholders by accumulating its earnings, provided that the accumulation is not unreasonable and is for a business purpose.

13. It is a separate legal "being," separate and apart from its owners (shareholders). It can be sued and can enter into contracts.

14. A corporation may own shares in another corporation and receive dividends, 85 percent of which are tax-free, subject to certain limitations.

Disadvantages of Incorporating

1. The owners of a corporation file two tax returns----individual and corporate. This may require added time and accounting expense. (The owner of a proprietorship files one return; a member of a partnership files two).

2. Unless the net taxable income from a business is substantial (i.e., $75,000 or more annually), there may not be tax advantages.

3. Maintaining the corporate records may require added time.

4. If debt financing is obtained by a corporation (i.e., a loan from a bank), the fund source may require the personal guarantee by the owner(s), thereby eliminating the limited liability advantage of a corporation, at least to the extent of the loan.

The Only Business Structure

But in reality, there is only one valid choice for any publisher today----a corporation!

It should be your very first step in setting up your publishing business.

There are many reasons why operating through a corporation is crucially important. As a reminder, these include:

- Protection against personal liability. You can limit your financial risk to whatever you put into your company when you incorporate. In a proprietorship or partnership you *personally* have unlimited liability. Your cars, home, savings and other assets are protected. For this reason alone, incorporation in this litigation-crazy society is imperative.

- You can get all kinds of tax and personal benefits such as the ability to set up favorable pension and profit-sharing plans for yourself.

- You have more tax options than in a proprietorship or partnership. And there are many more prudent reasons to incorporate.

Two books that I've written can make it simple and inexpensive for you to both incorporate and keep the important records you will need even if you have a one-person company.

- *How To Form Your Own Corporation Without a Lawyer for under $75,* $19.95 plus $3 shipping and handling . . .

- *The Complete Book of Corporate Forms* contains virtually all the forms you will ever need, complete with instructions to help you protect your valuable corporate status, $69.95 plus $5 shipping and handling . . .

You can order these books from Nicholas Direct, Inc., 19918 Gulf Boulevard #7, Indian Shores, FL 34635, telephone: 813-596-4966.

You can also contact a company I founded and sold. The name is The Company Corporation (TCC). You can call and incorporate on the telephone in eight minutes or less in any state in the U.S., although they specialize in the popular Delaware corporation. TCC will also provide a free information kit. Their toll-free telephone number is 800-542-2677. Make sure you refer to this book, and I assure you they will give you extra special attention!

I can't overemphasize the importance of incorporation. If for any reason you would prefer incorporation through a lawyer and don't object to their fees, which can run $250 to $2,000 for incorporation and $50 to $200 for each form, that is, of course, up to you. But no matter which route you select, by all means incorporate.

Raising Capital

As the owner of a valuable property (any saleable manuscript), you have the primary ingredient necessary to attract capital. While you do not need much capital to enter into a self-publishing venture, you will need some start-up money. And if you are willing to share some of the potential profits with others, you can approach the publishing of a book in an altogether different way.

There are thousands of capital sources. I wrote the book, 43 *Proven Ways To Raise Capital for Your Small Business*, available from Nicholas Direct, Inc., 19918 Gulf Boulevard #7, Indian Shores, FL 34635. It contains hundreds of sources of capital, classified by name, address, telephone number and individual to contact.

Capital in the business world can take the form of debt financing—a loan— or equity financing—the sale of stock in a business. Whichever form you choose and decide is the best for your business, the most important factor in raising capital is the preparation of a carefully written plan. An outline of such a plan is included in 43 *Proven Ways To Raise Capital for Your Small Business*.

Here are some areas of source capital that can help in your search.

Loans—through personal friends, relatives; or private investors might loan money to a new and promising company; a bank, finance company or a factory (who can use inventory as collateral).

Private Offering—To avoid expense and time involved in a Securities and Exchange Commission (SEC) registration, shares of stock can be offered in the corporation at a price-per-share that is determined by the director(s).

The number of people willing to pay the stock price has to be limited. No more than 25 people can be approached about investing in the corporation.

If more than 25 people are approached, there may be violations of federal and state SEC regulations regarding offerings of stock, for which there are severe penalties.

These regulations hold that an offering to any more than 25 people is a "public offering." This type of offering must be registered.

Intra-state Offering----Shares of stock in the corporation may be offered to residents within the boundaries of any one state. There is no limit to either the number of persons approached or who become the shareholders. Consult with an attorney who is knowledgeable in this area, and obtain the services of an account-ant to prepare an "Offering Circular" that describes the history, goals and purpose of the company, and shows its financial status.

Investors should sign a "subscription agreement" which states that the stock is being bought for *investment* and not for *resale*.

In all states, intra-state stock offerings must be registered with the state SEC.

Public Offerings----You can engage an underwriter who will guide the corporation toward filing a prospectus with the SEC for the purpose of selling shares in the corporation to the public. "Start-up" as well as established companies can raise substantial funds by selling a minority portion (less than 51 percent) of the corporation. If the amount of capital sought is $500,000 or less, the rules are simpler. When "going public," consult with an attorney well versed in SEC matters.

Setting Up Your Office

In the beginning, most business people start their offices in their homes. This is an obvious advantage because you eliminate the need to rent or lease expensive office space. You might want to rent a post office box if you prefer keeping your business mail separate.

The Home Office Deduction

Due to changes in the tax laws, setting up an office in your home and getting tax deductions will make it necessary for you to follow a few guidelines.

You can no longer put your desk in the guest room or sewing room and expect to take a deduction for it. The room you use as an office must be strictly business-related. If the IRS audits your return, they will disallow an office-in-the-home deduction if you have too many other things in that room not related to your business. It's better not to have a bed, chest of drawers, television or anything else in your office that wouldn't be in any other normal office. If you don't have a separate room now, partition off a part of your basement or recreation room which will be used strictly for business.

Equipment You Will Need

You will need a computer with desktop publishing capability or a typewriter, files and a calculator or adding machine. You will also need stationery and several different types of forms. Sometimes you can order a "package" of business stationery and business cards. You will also need some sort of bookkeeping system. And you must be meticulous about keeping records, especially if you are incorporated. If you keep records manually, your local office supply store has many different bookkeeping systems, and perhaps someone there will help you decide which one is best for you. Even better would be a bookkeeping system on your computer.

Other pieces of office equipment you need are a postage meter and postage scale. This will help you do your mailings, including the mailing of books and promotional materials.

And you will need a business phone. Whether or not you have a separate line installed depends largely on your circumstances, but it's preferable.

As soon as your budget allows, get a fax machine as well.

Tax Deductibles

Remember, business expenses are tax deductible, so keep accurate records, including mileage in your car and a log of long-distance calls.

Fulfilling Orders

When orders start arriving, you will need a method of fulfilling orders. Sometimes you can arrange with your printer to store your books and mail them out if you supply prepared labels. To cut down on that expense, you could store your books in your own home and handle the mailing yourself. When you type labels, keep a copy of them. In this way, you will be building a list of buyers of your book, which will be invaluable when your next book comes along. And when your list gets large enough, you can generate a large profitable income from list rentals to other noncompetitive mailers. In my former company, list rental income was over $500,000 a year!

This is the manual method. The office supply store has gummed labels that have carbon paper in between. Type the labels; affix the original label to the book carton or bag, and stick the carbon copy of the label to an index card. On the index card, note the method of payment (cash, check, money order), the date the order was received and the date you mailed the book out. Should someone write back saying they never received the book, you will be able to verify when you sent it and check with the post office.

When you can afford doing so, you can fully computerize the operation as well. Any good computer store or consultant can advise you.

Sometimes orders come in with no payment. Figure 8.2 is a sample letter you might send to customers in such a case.

Figure 8.2 Sample Letter: Missing Payment

Dear Customer:

We enclose your order for the following book which arrived without payment.

Title _____ Price _____ Postage/Handling_____

Please return a check or money order in the amount of $_____, along with your order, and the book will be mailed to you promptly. We enclose a self-addressed return envelope for your convenience.

Sincerely,

Customer Service Dept.

Sometimes a book you sent out will be returned as undeliverable. This could happen if the recipient's address is unclear or incomplete, or if the address is a rural route or a post office box. Figure 8.3 is a sample of the letter you would use in this case.

Figure 8.3 Sample Letter: Undeliverable Book

Dear Customer:

On __(date)__, the book _____(title)_____, which was sent to you at the above address, was returned to us marked _____(post office's notation)_____.

We will be happy to mail a second copy if you will send us an address where you will be assured of receiving the book.

Sincerely,

Customer Service Dept.

If you take personal checks in payment for books, it is probably inevitable that some of them occasionally will bounce. The best way to deal with the situation is to send them a letter similar to Figure 8.4.

Figure 8.4 Sample Letter: How To Handle Bounced Check

Dear Customer:

Re: PRODUCT OBTAINED WITHOUT PAYMENT

Your (check, money order), #___, dated _____, was returned to us by your bank marked (insufficient funds, etc.). You ordered the following book(s) which were sent to you on _____.

Title: _____

Title: _____

We assume this nonpayment is an oversight or an error on your part. However, this is a serious matter because a product has been obtained without payment.

Please forward the amount of $_____ promptly to avoid credit and legal action by a collection agent who handles all our bad checks, payment defaults and improper use of credit cards. Thank you.

Sincerely,

Credit Manager

Occasionally a book will not reach the recipient, and you will get a letter or call asking what happened to it. Some people simply get impatient and expect their books to arrive the day after they put their order in the mail. But others have a valid complaint. Figure 8.5 is a sample of a reply to this type of inquiry.

Figure 8.5 Sample Letter: Book Mailed but Not Received Yet

Dear Customer:

Thank you for your letter stating that you did not receive the following book(s) you ordered:

Title: _____

According to our records, this book was mailed to you on (date). Occasionally, the post office takes several weeks to deliver books. Also, fourth class book rate usually takes longer to arrive than first class mail. If by (date) you have not received your book, please return this letter to us, and enclose your correct address plus a copy of your canceled check or money order receipt. We will then be happy to send a second copy of the book.

We're sorry for any inconvenience this may have caused you.
Sincerely,
Customer Service Dept.

When selling books through the mail, always offer a money-back guarantee. People are less reluctant to purchase articles through the mail when they know they will get a refund if they are not completely satisfied.

There will inevitably be some refunds. Some readers may not be 100 percent happy with the book, or it didn't meet a certain need they may have had. If your percentage of refund requests is below five percent, you are in the normal range.

When you receive a refund request, you will need certain information for your records. This will be when and how they purchased the book. To be able to track returns, Figure 8.6 is a sample letter to a customer who requests a refund.

Figure 8.6 Sample Letter: Tracking Refunds

Dear Customer:

The book you returned, _____(title)_____, has been received. We wish to comply with our policy of making a prompt refund.

However, the original address label has been obliterated or removed. This label has a code containing information regarding how, when, where and at what price the book was purchased. Since other companies also sell our books, the buyer must obtain his or her refund from the selling company. Also, this book is drop-shipped for certain mail-order firms and sold through major credit card organizations.

If this book was purchased directly from our company, a photocopy of your canceled check is required for a cash refund, or the credit card number used, so that we may issue a credit rebate to the charge card company.

Sincerely,
Customer Service Dept.

You may be fortunate enough to start receiving orders for your book before it is even printed. To comply with postal regulations, unless you specify a specific shipping date in your offer, you must send a product which has been ordered and paid for within 30 days of receipt of the order. If you foresee any difficulty in meeting this requirement, you should send a letter such as the sample in Figure 8.7.

Figure 8.7 Sample Letter: Shipping Date Notification

Dear Customer:

Thank you for your order for _____(title)_____. We expect to ship on or before (date) . We appreciate your patience and will make every effort to see that you receive your book as soon as it is available.

If this is not satisfactory and you would like a refund instead, please notify us on the bottom of this letter, and we will promptly comply with your request.

Sincerely,

Customer Service Dept.

___ Please send refund as I'd rather not wait.

Some customers may not be willing to wait that long and will ask for their money back. Still, remember that a customer who knows what to expect is much better satisfied than one who is not kept informed. Most people will be happy to wait if you communicate with them.

Chapter 9

You as Publisher: Important Considerations

Y ou will need to consider a few more things before beginning your publishing business. These deal with fulfillment of orders.

P. O. Box versus Street Address

While there are differing views on the question of using a post office box or receiving orders in your home, I recommend a street address. Many people mistrust a company whose only address is listed as a post office box. In mail order selling, it is important to continually build credibility. Some people who have had bad experiences with mail order companies are wary of new ones.

A street address suggests that your company has more substance and stability than a numbered box. You can use your home address, an office or a mail forwarding service. The latter will be the best in terms of protecting your privacy and preventing book buyers from showing up at your house. But a home or office address will get your orders to you faster. An added benefit of receiving your own mail is that the likelihood of orders being lost or misplaced is diminished.

179

Fulfillment Procedures

Prior to receiving orders for your book, you should carefully organize procedures for filling them. It is most discouraging to a book buyer when there is a long delay in shipment. Prompt shipments on same day received or within 24 hours are desirable for a successful operation.

Here are suggestions for processing orders:

Mailing Cartons

To protect your book against damage during shipment, use a cushioned bag or sturdy carton. Many printers and/or stationery stores stock them. Sometimes it's advantageous to have your book packaged in mailing cartons through the printer who produces the book.

Labels

For a manual operation addressing the book, use a gummed or pressure-sensitive, four-part label. Your stationer will have these; they come with an original and three copies. There are usually 33 labels per sheet. Use one for your customer's address, which goes on the mailing carton. The first carbon copy is to keep in compiling a list of your customers. The other two copies are for possible future mailings to your customers, and extra file copies. Type the department code (key number) and the date of shipment on the label, for reference in the event there is correspondence about the order.

For computer operation, you merely devise a similar system.

Nondelivery Complaints

If a customer writes to tell you that he or she has not received the book after 30 days of receipt of order, send another book immediately at no cost. The post office does fail to deliver on occasion, and it is not worth the hassle to try to determine if this is actually the case. There are, within direct marketing, a minority of "rip-off" artists who defraud companies of merchandise through the mail. Fortunately, these people are rare, especially in selling information products. It is much less of a headache to simply send another book than to lose the good will of an honest customer.

Fourth Class Book Rate

Have your company name and address and the words "Books—Special Fourth Class Rate" printed directly on your mailing carton or shipping bag, or on a printed label. You will then qualify for this low-cost postal rate.

Storing Your Books

Keep inventory in your home, or rent a small warehouse space until your printings become large. At that point have your printer warehouse your books, or rent a larger warehouse. You will have to pay a storage fee for this service. Many printers will fill orders for you, usually at a nominal fee, if you provide the prepared labels and postage costs. No matter how large your business becomes, keep a supply of your books on hand to send Air Mail, Special Delivery, or to give as complimentary or review copies.

Hiring Helpers

When you begin doing a volume business, you will need help in this important fulfillment function. It is here that most of your customers will get their first (and lasting) impression of you and how you do business. If they must wait weeks to receive their books while hearing nothing from you in the interim, you risk several things. Namely, canceling their orders, returning the books for refunds when they finally do arrive, and calling the Better Business Bureau, Federal Trade Commission (FTC) or consumer protection agencies and complaining to other people who could be good future buyers of your products. *Don't* let this happen. When the workload becomes too much for you to handle, bring in some outside help. You can do this in several ways:

    a. Hire on a salaried basis.

    b. Hire on a part-time, hourly basis.

    c. Hire a self-employed independent contractor.

At Nicholas Direct, we use a combination of these methods. We employ a former employee who works from her home. She is paid on a per-order basis. This arrangement works very well.

If this appeals to you, you could work out such an arrangement by running a classified ad in your local paper. Also, watch for ads under the "Services Offered" and "Situation Wanted" classifications.

I consider hiring employees a *marketing* function, not a personnel matter, as it is handled in most companies. Dedicated, loyal and productive employees will help you build a profitable business.

Here is an ad I recently ran which produced 117 highly qualified candidates:

Executive Secretary. Busy writer seeks best secretary on Gulf Coast. Top office skills including editing ability required. Media or publishing background helpful. Challenging position, great working conditions. Salary open. Write to Mr. Nicholas, 19918 Gulf Blvd. Unit 7, Indian Shores, FL 34635.

The Independent Contractor

An incentive pay scale for an independent contractor could be set up along these lines: processing individual book orders at $1 a piece with a mutually agreed upon hourly rate for miscellaneous services on your behalf.

You can establish arrangements that best suit your needs and the general pay scale of the area in which you live. When someone is paid on an incentive basis, they tend to work efficiently because it means they will make more money in the shortest amount of time.

Join the Better Business Bureau

To help establish your credibility in the public's eye in your own community and with your customers, join the Better Business Bureau (BBB). People feel better dealing with a firm that is accepted by the business community and that works hard to maintain certain standards of fairness and established business practices. Although you cannot use this agency's name or symbol in your advertising, you will receive a plaque which you can display in your office. You will also be kept abreast of current developments in consumer protection areas, be allowed to vote on certain policies and have a voice in issues that affect your business. My companies have been members of the Better Business Bureau since their inception.

You might also consider joining the Chamber of Commerce in your town or city. This is another important organization, and often it is the source of some very good free publicity for your business.

Keeping Records

The best advice I can give you in the area of recordkeeping is to start out correctly in the very beginning. Doing it right from the start of your business will allow things to run more smoothly and will make it easier for you to turn over your books to a bookkeeper or accountant when the time comes.

The temptation is to begin paying bills and stick receipts in desk drawers with the idea that "I'll-get-organized-as-soon-as-I-have-some-time." That will never happen, of course, at least not before you have to beg an accountant or bookkeeper to put your long-out-dated and incomplete records into accounting language. If you procrastinate on the matter of recordkeeping for even the shortest time, it will cost dearly when the time comes to do your taxes and hire an accountant to piece together the financial history of your business.

Also, if you fail to keep accurate records, how are you going to measure performance? How will you be able to plan for tax time by making prudent purchases at the right times and investing your profits in more inventory? You will need to keep accurate records, or you may face stiff penalties from the IRS, especially if you have paid employees.

In the beginning, hire an accountant or bookkeeper who moonlights for very little money. He or she will maintain a set of books that will tell you exactly where your business venture stands at any given point in time. Get some accountant recommendations from local business people.

The "One-Write" System

The simplest manual method I've found for keeping records is a "one-write" system. With this, you write a check, and the check is automatically posted to your ledger through a sheet of carbon paper. You also write the address on the check and use a handy window envelope, eliminating the need for writing the address twice. One good supplier of the system is the Safeguard Co., found in your Yellow Pages.

If you use this system and enter all the bills you pay, you will have the basis of a good accounting system. Accounts Receivable, Accounts Payable and journals are also available to keep track of your receipts, receivables and cash expenditures.

Keeping Track of Orders

You will also need a manual or computerized method of keeping track of your orders on a per-key-number basis. You've already seen how to prepare an analysis of your book sales in terms of their profitability, but usually you prepare this report only once a week at the most. You will need a method of posting the daily receipts to provide the information for the analysis. Figure 9.1 is a sample of the sheets Nicholas Direct uses, with full explanation of their use.

Figure 9.1 Sample Method for Keeping Track of Orders

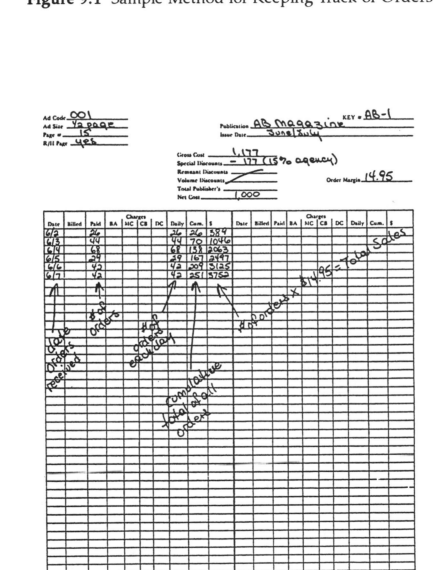

On this sheet you will notice spaces to record orders on credit cards and "billed" orders. Offering an option for charging the purchase on a credit card increases your number of orders substantially. To obtain more information about becoming authorized to accept credit card charges, speak with your banker.

If you are denied what is called a merchant credit card status, it may be possible to set up arrangements with a second company, such as those that advertise in *USA Today*.

You will need to offer the credit card option to your customers to achieve real volume sales.

Toll-Free Number

As soon as feasible, arrange to have a toll-free number: either in your office or through an outside service bureau. Your customers have come to expect this option which is provided by nearly all direct marketers.

Credit Selling

Another area that you might try is allowing your buyers to be billed for their purchases. However, you will need far more working capital, and it could result in bad debts of 20 percent to as high as 50 percent, depending on the list or media you use. Credit selling involves more paperwork. You are probably better off without it, at least in the early stages of publishing. If you wish to pursue it, first you must set up methods of screening the orders. For example, it has been the experience of many businesses that people listing their addresses as post office boxes are best avoided.

Running Credit Checks

You can join a credit reporting agency which has lists of mail order buyers. There is a charge for each name you submit for credit clearance, and the agency will send you a report about that customer's credit-worthiness. Unfortunately, a lot of people will

186

order something on a "bill me later" basis and simply not pay for it. Avoid "bill me later" offers until your company is solidly on its feet. While the "bill me later" option may seem to significantly increase sales, it may turn out that your return rate and bad debts are higher and serve to offset the sales you made in the beginning.

If you decide to go into credit selling later on, make certain, once again, that your recordkeeping is impeccable. If you get an order from a "deadbeat" or someone who does not pay, mark this information on your computerized mailing list or your index card bearing his or her address label. Don't make the mistake of sending them another order.

At Nicholas Direct, we have found that the return rate on cash orders is so low (less than two percent) that we would rather have fewer orders and a low return rate than many more orders and correspondingly high return and bad debt rates. However, we have used credit selling very successfully at certain times in the past. We will undoubtedly do so again in the future.

Other Ways To Make Money from Your Book

Paperback Reprint Rights
If your advertising and promotion efforts are successful, you might want to contact a conventional publisher with your sales figures in hand. You can sometimes generate a five- or even six-figure advance sale through selling the paperback rights to your book. Even with a cheaper paperback on the market, sales and demand for the hardbound copy often do not diminish! So you can in most cases keep selling your direct mail edition for as long as it is profitable.

Foreign Rights
Again, after your sales success in this country, contact a book agent who handles foreign rights. Rights to publish your book can be sold throughout the world. Thousands of authors add to both their finances and prestige through this method.

Two questions should be answered before you attempt sales in other countries. First, as mentioned before, is your book selling in the U.S.? Second, does it lend itself to use by readers in other countries?

For example, a book on *How To Obtain a Divorce in Reno, Nevada* would not be useful to international readers. However, a book on the *Secrets of Organic Gardening* might very well be popular throughout the world.

A knowledgeable agent will be the best judge of your book's potential market overseas and whether or not there are similar books published in other countries.

Rights to several of my books have been sold in Poland, China, Germany, France, Canada, Switzerland, Czechoslovakia and Hungary, to name a few. It's a real thrill to see a book that I've written or published produced and sold in another country!

Book Clubs

Another group who you might interest in rights to your book are book clubs. There can be sizeable royalties involved in a major book club contract. They will buy your copies from you outright (with a return privilege), they will share in a print run, or they will purchase rights to the manuscript and produce their own editions of your book. LMP is the best source of names and addresses for book clubs. A good "pitch" letter is essential in this case. Tell the person exactly WHY your book would be good for their members and how well it will fit into their line. Send all the promotional literature you have along with a copy of the book.

Making Money from Your Mailing List

Another way to make money from book sales involves your mailing list. A side benefit of developing your own mailing list is that many others will pay handsomely to use your list for selling their products. When you order through the mail, you have undoubtedly received an increasing amount of direct mail from other companies. This is because the original company from whom you ordered a product has rented your name and address to other companies.

Contrary to what some believe, most people who are accustomed to buying products through the mail like to receive the opportunity to buy more. Buying through the mail is a great convenience and saves a lot of money.

If you develop a list of book buyers who would be good prospects for other companies, you can rent the list to mail order merchandisers of similar products. For instance, if your book was an organic gardening topic, merchandisers of seeds, garden tools, plants, outdoor clothing and health foods would probably be interested.

If you think another company would be interested in renting your list (and they would need at least 3,000–5,000 names in the beginning), write to that company's marketing department. You might even send them a copy of your book along with copies of your ads and direct mail letters. Lists usually rent for about $75–$115 per thousand names, and the names need to be available on a computer printout.

Handling mailing list rentals usually involves a little time, but it can be one of your most profitable sources of income, bringing you a five- or six-figure annual income.

The List Broker's Role

I recommend hiring a reputable direct mail list broker. Names and addresses are available in *Direct Marketing Magazine*, which should be in your library. Once having engaged a broker, you will receive a copy of all orders for your list.

Should a company be interested in renting your list, always request and receive a sample of the proposed mailing before you give them permission to use it. If the offer is going to be competitive with yours or is not in good taste, don't rent them your list.

Keeping an Eye on Competitors

Keep an eye on competitors. You may find that someone is copying elements of your book. This happened to one of my books, and it is a very serious legal problem. Not only does it involve plagiarism, but in most cases it is a violation of federal copyright laws. Make sure your work is copyrighted properly as soon as possible. Make every effort to keep on top of other publisher's products. If you see anyone copying your work without authorization, see a good lawyer immediately.

"Seeding" Your List

"Seed" your mailing list with names and addresses of friends or relatives who are willing to send you mail received from your list renters. It's easy to identify by your friends if their names are spelled differently on your list. You will then be receiving all the mailings from companies who have used your list. You can then monitor the usage and also determine if anyone ever uses your list who has not been authorized to do so.

Remaindering Your Book

Remaindering is a subject that may seem a bit negative to include in a book about creating a bestseller. But it is a subject that we can't overlook as you should know about it. If any book you publish simply isn't selling despite all your efforts, remainder it. This is big business, and there is a big market for these books. Sometimes books are remaindered because they are overstocked. Sometimes the publisher came out with a new, updated edition of a book which made the previous edition obsolete, but still had an inventory of the old edition. Sometimes they are books that were returned by bookstores. There are many reasons for remaindering books, not all of them bad or indicative of a book's failure to sell.

Should you decide that this is a course you would like to pursue, contact several remainder buyers (they are listed in *Publishers Weekly*

190

and *Literary Market Place*). Include the following information: binding (hardcover, paperback), retail price, publication date, number of copies sold, your name, address and phone number. Send them a copy of the book. Ask for an offer. Sometimes you can get a good price for your books (ranging from actual printing costs to 50 percent of the retail price), but the most common offers are in the 20-cents-a-book range. But this is better than nothing. And you get them out of your storage area, which can reduce cost.

When remaindering, negotiate the best deal possible. You are not a giant publisher paying large fees for warehousing inventory. You can afford to bargain.

Chapter 10

A Word about Special Subject Books

Up to this point, I've been addressing primarily books appealing to a vast audience. What if your book has a limited market?

This, in itself, should not deter you from publishing. The important thing is to know your market and to aggressively expose your book to it. Let's look at an example.

Suppose you've written a book outlining the biographies of famous (and infamous) cowboys, gunfighters and others responsible for the "taming" of the "Wild West." Most people would call it a limited-market or special-interest book. But even though there is no mass audience, there are many people who will be interested. Thousands of "Wild West" buffs would welcome a book like this, if it is well written, to add to their collections.

To market the book, the first thing to do is visit the local library. Take a look at the other books on the subject, and note the publishers. Then contact those publishers, inquiring about their mailing lists. If they don't maintain a list in-house, they will usually give the name of their list broker. Sometimes books like this are not marketed through the mail at all but rather to bookstores and libraries. The publisher will tell you if this is the case.

Next, check in LMP for the names and addresses of special publications, such as magazines catering to "Wild West" buffs, Western lore, horses and saddlery, historical societies, antique gun collectors, memorabilia collectors, antiquarian societies and clubs. Also check for male-oriented publications. With a book like this, your major audience will probably be male, so aim for them.

Your next step would be to list the names and addresses of "fringe audience" publications. Since this particular book's fringe audience will be (possibly) men interested in action stories and such, and retired people who might remember the "old days," prepare a list of publications catering to these groups. Other magazines that men typically read would be the how-to-do-it science and mechanics magazines and business magazines. Another fringe market might be the nostalgic audience—the people who are interested in collecting books about and articles from times past. Still another fringe audience category might be those people who are interested in crime and criminals.

As you can see, the possibilities are many. Don't assume that because you have a unique subject, you automatically have a limited market. It's too tough for anyone to know in advance the scope of the market for any book. In my experience, a long shot sometimes turns out better than the ones that seem to be sure winners.

Fiction and poetry are more difficult subjects to direct market successfully, mainly because these subjects are normally purchased through bookstores, libraries, trade distributors and book clubs. However, it is not impossible. Do some research and investigation into your potential markets. Decide which market might be best for your book, and plan to market it accordingly.

Technical and scientific writing is another area where you can publish. Take some extra time to ferret out the appropriate audience. If you are willing to put forth the effort, you will find it.

With all limited-market subjects, here's a tip: Don't be swayed by the price breaks you can obtain with large first printings. Start small, see how the sales are going and make sure you are able to market the book before investing a great deal of money in inventory. Subsequent printings are always cheaper (when plates have been made), and it is usually no problem at all to get a "rush" order through for a second or third printing. If your book takes off, you can go into subsequent printings easily. If the book starts off selling slowly and needs further market research to get it going, you have not invested a large sum of money, nor are you paying for warehouse space.

Afterword

If you follow the guidelines of this book, you can publish any book or saleable information product and make it a bestseller.

My aim is to help you save money, improve your skills and live a more successful, happier and even healthier life. Your lifestyle will also undoubtedly improve. Publishing has the potential to help bring you all of these things and much more.

When you learn to apply your individual talents which are so unique to you, you can achieve all the things your activities can make possible.

After your book is published (or your information product marketed), I'd appreciate a short note and an autographed copy of your book or video or Special Report, etc., along with any comments you may have. (I already have a library full of them, and they are precious possessions.)

I plan from time to time to revise and update this book. If you have any suggestions for improvement in any area, I'd certainly welcome them.

To your happiness and success,

Ted Nicholas

Appendix

Printers, Book Manufacturers, Video and Audio Producers

Adams Press
500 North Michigan Ave. #1920
Chicago, IL 60011
Tel: 312-236-3838

Banta Company, Inc.
Curtis Reed Plaza
P. O. Box 60
Menasha, WI 54952
Tel: 414-722-7771

Bok Industries, Inc. (Binders)
11 Kent Dr.
Hockessin, DE 19707

The Book Press
Div. of Quebecor America, Inc.
Plant: Putney Rd.
Brattleboro, VT 05301
Tel: 802-257-7701

Braceland Brothers, Inc. (Books)
7625 Suffolk Ave.
Philadelphia, PA 19153
Tel: 215-492-0200

The R. L. Bryan Company
Box 368
Greystone Executive Park
Columbia, SC 29202
Tel: 803-779-3560

Capital City Press (Books)
1841 Forest Dr.
Williamstown, NJ 08094
Tel: 609-875-5654
Capital City Press
Customer Service
P. O. Box 546, Airport Dr.
Berlin, VT 05602
Tel: 802-223-6810

Century Graphics
(Newsletters, Updates)
3020 Darnell Rd.
Philadelphia, PA 19154

John H. Dekker & Sons, Inc.
2941 Clydon St. SW
Grand Rapids, MI 49509
Tel: 616-538-5160

R. R. Donnelley & Sons Co.
77 West Wacker Dr.
Chicago, IL 60601
Tel: 312-326-8000

Eastern Litho (Books)
2815 North 17th St.
Philadelphia, PA 19132

Farley Printing Co, Inc.
(Books, Newsletters)
115 South Justison .St.
Wilmington, DE 19801

Graphic Composition, Inc.
Div. of The Heritage Group
240 Hawthorne Ave.
Athens, GA 30606
Tel: 404-546-8688

Graphic Reproductions
(Books, Newsletters)
1957 Pioneer Rd. Bldg. F
Huntingdon Valley, PA 19006
Tel: 215-957-6120

D. B. Hess Company (Books)
350 West Passail St.
Rochelle Park, NJ 07662

Maple-Vale Co., Inc.
Box 2695
Willow Springs Ln.
York, PA 17405
Tel: 717-764-5911

Maple-Vale Book Mfg. Group
Pine Camp Dr.
P. O. Box 1005
Binghamton, NY 13902

Multiprint, Inc.
80 Longhill Ln.
Chatham, NJ 07928
Tel: 201-635-6400

Optic Graphics (Books)
101 Dover Rd.
Glen Burnie, MD 21061

Pantagraph Printing &
Stationery Co.
217 West Jefferson St.
Bloomington, IL 61702
Tel: 309-829-1071

Publishers' Book Bindery, Inc.
21 East St.
Winchester, MA 01890
Tel: 617-729-8000

Quadra Graphics (Books)
7120 Airport Highway
Pennsauken, NJ 08109
Tel: 609-665-4060

Rose Printing Co., Inc.
2503 Jackson Bluff Rd.
Box 5078
Tallahassee, FL 32314
Tel: 904-576-4151

Smith-Edwards-Dunlap Co.
2867 East Allegheny Ave.
  at Delaware Expwy.
Philadelphia, PA 19134
Tel: 215-425-8800

Stackpole Press
Box 1831
Cameron & Kelker St.
Harrisburg, PA 17105
Tel: 717-234-5091

Standard Forms
602 Newark Shopping Center
Newark, DE 19711
Tel: 800-688-1275

Taylor Publishing Co.
1550 West Mockingbird Ln.
Box 597
Dallas, TX 75235
Tel: 214-637-2800

Velo-Bind, Inc.
901 Mariner's Island Blvd. #285
San Mateo, CA 94404
Tel: 415-571-0200

Versa Press (Books)
R. R. 1, Spring Bay Rd.
P. O. Box 2460
East Peoria, IL 61611-0460
Tel: 309-822-8272

**Vicks Lithograph
& Printing Corp.**
Box 2701 Commercial Dr.
Yorkville, NY 13495
Tel: 315-736-9346

Von-Hoffman Press, Inc.
1000 Camera Ave.
St. Louis, MO 63126
Tel: 314-966-0909

Western Publishing Co., Inc.
1220 Mount Ave.
Racine, WI 53404
Tel: 414-633-2431

Wickersham Printing (Books)
2959 Old Tree Dr.
Lancaster, PA 17603

Book Review Syndicates

John Barkham Reviews
27 East 65 St.
New York, NY 10021
Tel: 212-879-9705

Feature News Service
2330 South Brentwood Blvd.
St. Louis, MO 63144
Tel: 314-961-2300

King Features Syndicate
235 East 45 St.
New York, NY 10017
Tel: 212-455-4000

National Catholic News Service
3211 Fourth St. NE
Washington, DC 20017
Tel: 202-541-3250

George H. Tweney
16660 Marine View Dr. SW
Seattle, WA 98166
Tel: 206-243-8243

United Press International
1400 I St. NW
Washington, DC 20005
Tel: 202-898-8000

Courses for the Book Trade

Various courses are given each year covering different phases of the book trade and graphic arts. Among the institutions and associations sponsoring such courses are the ones listed below. Detailed information can be obtained by writing directly to the universities or associations.

Columbia University
Writing Div. Sch. of the Arts
404 Dodge Hall
Columbia University
New York, NY 10027
Tel: 212-854-4391
Graduate writing program. Two-year course leading to the MFA degree. Seminars and workshops in poetry, fiction, nonfiction.

Graphic Arts Education Center
Graphic Arts Association
1900 Cherry St.
Philadelphia, PA 19103
Tel: 215-299-3300

Hunter College
School of General Studies
(Adult Ed. Programs Center
for Lifelong Learning)
695 Park Ave.
New York, NY 10021
Tel: 212-772-4490

Institute of Early American History
Box 220
Williamsburg, VA 23187
Tel: 804-221-1110

Mystery Writers of America
236 West 27th St. #600
New York, NY 10001
Tel: 212-255-7005

New York City Technical College
300 Jay St.
Brooklyn, NY 11201
Tel: 718-260-5000

New York University
Center for Publishing
School of Continuing Education
48 Cooper Square #108
New York, NY 10003
Tel: 212-998-7220

Northwestern University
Medill School of Journalism
Fisk Hall - 1813 Hinman
Evanston, IL 60208
Tel: 708-491-5665

Ohio University
English Dept.
385 Ellis Hall
Creative Writing Program
Athens, OH 45701
Tel: 614-593-2838

Radcliffe College/Harvard
Radcliffe's Publishing Course
77 Brattle St.
Cambridge, MA 02138
Tel: 617-495-8678

Rochester Institute of Technology
School of Printing
One Lomb Memorial Dr.
Rochester, NY 14623
Tel: 716-475-2727

Stanford University
Stanford Alumni Association
Bowman House
Box LMP
Stanford, CA 94305
Tel: 415-725-1083

School of Visual Arts
209 East 23 St.
New York, NY 10010
Tel: 212-679-7350

Simmons College
300 The Fenway
Boston, MA 02115
Syracuse University
Syracuse, NY 13244-2100
Tel: 315-443-2302

University of Wisconsin
Madison Communications Program
Journalism & Mass Comm. Dept.
226 Lowell Hall
610 Langdon St.
Madison, WI 53703
Tel: 608-262-3982

Direct Mail Specialists

The AARDVARK Group
Div. of HOME Corp.
9380 Hidden Lake Cr.
Dexter, MI 48130
Tel: 313-426-5755

ADirect, Inc.
95 Oser Ave.
Hauppauge, NY 11788
Tel: 212-807-0048

Cerulli Communications, Inc.
56 Glendale Rd.
Ossining, NY 10562
Tel: 914-762-0644

Conrad Direct, Inc.
80 West St.
Englewood, NJ 07631
Tel: 201-567-3200

Creative AD/Ventures, Inc.
2648 Grand Ave.
Bellmore, NY 11710
Tel: 516-679-1701

D & D Associates
133 Bayberry Ln
New Rochelle, NY 10804
Tel: 914-835-0900

Direct Mail Promotions, Inc.
Co-Operative Mailing Div.
18 East 41st St. #1605
New York, NY 10017
Tel: 212-370-7998

Ecocenters Corp.
21111 Chagrin Blvd.
Beachwood, OH 44122
Tel: 216-991-9000

Freelance Express, Inc.
111 East 85th St.
New York, NY 10028
Tel: 212-427-0331

Friedman Harris & Partners
125 Wireless Blvd.
Hauppauge, NY 11788
Tel: 516-231-1431

Garden State Business Forms, Inc.
18 Passaic Ave.
Fairfield, NJ 07004
Tel: 201-808-0008

Lazarus Marketing, Inc.
3530 Oceanside Rd.
Oceanside, NY 11572
Tel: 516-678-5107

Mailbag, Inc.
3041 Marwin Ave.
Bensalem, PA 19020-6524
Tel: 215-244-4440

Publishers Marketing Association
2401 Pacific Coast Hwy. #102
Hermosa Beach, CA 90254
Tel: 213-372-2732

Jack Schecterson Associates
5316-251st Pl.
Little Neck, NY 11362
Tel: 718-225-3536

Wiland Services, Inc.
6707 Winchester Cr.
Boulder, CO 80301-3598
Tel: 303-530-0606

Wholesalers To Bookstores

The Baker & Taylor Co.
Box 6920, 625 East Main St.
Bridgewater, NJ 08807-0920
Tel: 908-218-0400
<u>Western Division:</u>
380 Edison Way
Reno, NV 89564-0099
Tel: 702-786-6700
V.P. & Gen. Mgr. Jim Plecker
<u>Southeast Division:</u>
Mount Olive Rd.
Commerce, GA 30599
Tel: 404-334-5000
V.P. & Gen. Mgr. Carol Osborne

Bookazine Co., Inc.
330 West 10th St.
New York, NY 10014
Tel: 212-675-8877
Pres.: Erwin Kallman

Bookpeople, Inc.
2929 Fifth St.
Berkeley, CA 94710
Tel: 4150549-3030
Pres.: Miriam Foley

DeVorss & Co., Inc.
Box 550
Marina Del Ray, CA 90294
Tel: 213-870-7478

Ingram Book Company
Div. of Ingram Dist. Group, Inc.
1125 Heil Quaker Blvd.
LaVergne, TN 37086
Tel: 615-793-5000

International Publications Service
114 East 32nd St.
New York, NY 10016
Tel: 212-685-9351
Gen. Mgr.: William C. Collings

International Service Company
333 Fourth Ave.
Indialantic, FL 32903
Tel: 407-724-1443
Pres.: Dennis Samuels

Knowledge, Inc.
3863 Southwest Loop 280 #100
Fort Worth, TX 76133-2063
Tel: 817-292-4270

Milligan News Co., Inc.
150 North Autumn St.
San Jose, CA 96110
Tel: 408-286-7604

X-S Books, Inc.
95 Mayhill Rd.
Saddlebrook, NJ 07662
Tel: 201-712-9266

Artists and Art Services

Design Element
8624 Wonderland Ave.
Los Angeles, CA 90046
Tel: 213-656-3293
Book, jacket and poster design,
cartoons, illustration, spot drawings,
letterheads, trademarks, photography,
charts and graphs, brochures.

Adrianne Onderdonk Dudden
829 Old Gulph Rd.
Bryn Mawr, PA 19010
Tel: 215-525-6584
Book and jacket design, illustration.
Trade, text and art books.

Gary Gore
1913 Blair Blvd.
Nashville, TN 37205
Tel: 615-298-3588
Book and jacket design, layout,
letterheads, trademarks. Specialist in
art, scholarly and technical books.

Philip Grushkin, Inc.
86 East Linden Ave.
Englewood, NJ 07631
Tel: 201-568-6686
Book and jacket design, layout,
letterheads, lettering, trademarks,
calligraphy, map and poster design,
complete production.

Repro Art Service
102 Swinick Dr.
Dunmore, PA 18512
Tel: 717-961-5410
Dir.: Angelo Rinaldi
Book and jacket design, retouching,
spot drawings, trademarks, illustration
dummying, layout and mechanicals,
audio visual.

John Seitz
6902 Commerce Ave.
Port Richey, FL 34668
Tel: 813-842-4682
Graphic Designer

Kelly Solis-Navarro
1051 Santa Cruz Ave.
Menlo Park, CA 94025
Tel: 415-322-6937
Book, exhibit, jacket and poster design,
illustration layout, letterheads,
lettering, retouching, spot drawings,
trademarks, charts and graphs.

Sandy Taccone
16 Vane Ct.
New Castle, DE 19720
Tel: 302-323-0343
Graphic Designer

Mrs. Lili Cassel Wronker
144-44 Village Rd.
Jamaica, NY 11435
Tel: 718-380-3990
Graphic Designer
Illustration, jacket, map and poster
design, layout, letterheads, lettering,
spot drawings, trademarks, typography,
photography.

Book Review Services

AB Bookman's Weekly
Box AB
Clifton, NJ 07015
Tel: 201-772-0020

**Appraisal: Science Books
for Young People**
Boston Univ. School of Education
605 Commonwealth Ave.
Boston, MA 02215
Tel: 617-353-4150

Book Review Digest
H. W. Wilson Co.
950 University Ave.
Bronx, NY 10452
Tel: 800-367-6770

The Booklist
American Library Association
50 East Huron St.
Chicago, IL 60611
Tel: 312-944-6780

**Bulletin of the Center
for Children's Books**
University of Chicago
1100 East 57th St.
Chicago, IL 60637
Tel: 312-702-8284

Choice
Association of College
 & Research Libraries
100 Riverview Center
Middletown, CT 06457
Tel: 203-347-6933

The Horn Book Magazine
Horn Book, Inc.
14 Beacon St.
Boston, MA 02108
Tel: 617-227-1555

The Kirkus Review
200 Park Ave. S
New York, NY 10003
Tel: 212-777-4554

**Kliatt Young Adult Paperback
Book Guide**
425 Watertown St.
Newton, MA 02158
Tel: 617-965-4666

Law Books in Review
Glanville Publishers
75 Main St.
Dobbs Ferry, NY 10522
Tel: 914-693-1320

Library Journal
Cahners Publishing Co.
249 West 17th St.
New York, NY 10011
Tel: 212-463-6822

Medievalia et Humanistica
Box 13348, North Texas Univ.
Denton, TX 76203
Tel: 817-565-2050

New York Review of Books
250 West 57th St.
New York, NY 10107
Tel: 212-757-8070

Publishers Weekly-Forecasts
249 West 17th St.
New York, NY 10011
Tel: 212-563-6758

Reprint Bulletin-Book Reviews
Glanville Publishers, Inc.
75 Main St.
Dobbs Ferry, NY 10522
Tel: 914-693-1320

The Review of Education
Box 786
Cooper Station
New York, NY 10276
Tel: 212-206-8900

Reviews in American History
701 West 40th St. #275
Baltimore, MD 21211
Tel: 301-338-6990

Reviews in Anthropology
Box 786
Cooper Station
New York, NY 10276
Tel: 212-206-8900

School Library Journal
249 West 17th St.
New York, NY 10011
Tel: 212-463-6759

Books by Ted Nicholas

The Complete Book of Corporate Forms

The Complete Guide to Business Agreements

The Complete Guide to Consulting Success (coauthor, Howard Shenson)

The Complete Guide to Nonprofit Corporations

The Complete Guide to "S" Corporations

The Executive's Business Letter Book

43 Proven Ways To Raise Capital for Your Small Business

The Golden Mailbox: How To Get Rich Direct Marketing Your Product

How To Form Your Own Corporation Without a Lawyer for under $75

How To Gain Financial Freedom as an Independent Contractor

How To Get a Top Job in Tough Times

How To Publish a Book and Sell a Million Copies

Investment Strategies for Business Owners

Secrets of Entrepreneurial Leadership: Building Top Performance Through Trust and Teamwork

The Ted Nicholas Small Business Course

Your Handbook to a Successful Home-Based Business

Recommended Reading

Title	Author
How To Make Your Advertising Make Money	John Caples
Making Ads Pay	John Caples
Tested Advertising Methods	John Caples
Robert Collier Letter Book	Robert Collier
Eicoff on Broadcast Direct Marketing	Alvin Eicoff
The Art of Clear Thinking	Rudolph Fleisch
How To Make Maximum Money in Minimum Time	Gary Halbert
Direct Mail and Mail Order Handbook	Richard Hodgson
The Greatest Direct Mail Sales Letters of All Times	Richard Hodgson
My Life in Advertising/Scientific Advertising	Claude Hopkins
The Lazy Man's Way to Riches	Joe Karbo
The Lasker Story as He Told It	Albert Lasker
The Golden Mailbox	Ted Nicholas
Confessions of an Advertising Man	David Oglivy
Oglivy on Advertising	David Oglivy
Reality in Advertising	Rosser Reeves
101 Tips for More Profitable Catalogues	Maxwell Saog

How To Write a Good Advertisement   Vic Schwab

Successful Direct Marketing Methods   Bob Stone

The 100 Greatest Advertisements   Julian Watkins

NOTE: A good source of these books. Catalog is available. Carl Galletti, One Paddock Drive, Lawrenceville, NJ 08648-1566, telephone 609-896-0245, fax 609-896-2653.

Index

About the Author

Ted Nicholas is a multifaceted business personality. In addition to being a well-known author and respected speaker, Mr. Nicholas remains an active participant in his own entrepreneurial ventures. Without capital, he started his first business at age 21. Since then, he has started 22 companies of his own.

Mr. Nicholas has written and/or published 52 books on business and finance since his writing career began in 1972. The best know is *How To Form Your Own Corporation Without a Lawyer for under $75*. His previous business enterprises include Peterson's House of Fudge, a candy and ice cream manufacturing business conducted through 30 retail stores, as well as other businesses in franchising, real estate, machinery and food.

When the author was only 29, he was selected by a group of business leaders as one of the most outstanding businessmen in the nation and was invited to the White House to meet the President.

Although Mr. Nicholas has founded many successful enterprises, he also has experienced two major setbacks and many minor ones. He considers business setbacks necessary to success and the only true way to learn anything in life, a lesson that goes all the way back to childhood. That's why he teaches other entrepreneurs how to "fail forward."

Mr. Nicholas has appeared on numerous television and radio shows and conducts business seminars in Florida and Switzerland. Presently, he owns and operates four corporations of his own and acts as marketing consultant and copywriter to small as well as large businesses.

Build Wealth with the Latest Timely Information on Self-Publishing and Direct Marketing

Imagine getting the inside information on the very latest self-publishing and direct marketing breakthroughs each and every month!

Ted Nicholas writes a monthly newsletter, entitled *The Ted Nicholas Letter*, available exclusively to his subscribers. Here are a few of the areas covered:

- The hottest book topics to write and publish.
- The latest trends and how to cash in on them in marketing strategies.
- The latest on headlines and book titles that pull sales.
- The most productive new mailing lists.
- The magazines that pay out best for your ads.
- Places to get free advertising and publicity, including radio, TV and magazines.
- Invaluable contacts to help your publishing business grow.
- New copywriting discoveries that work.

A yearly subscription to *The Ted Nicholas Letter* is only $277, tax deductible. And you have an unconditional money-back guarantee. If at any time you wish to cancel your subscription, you will receive a refund on all remaining issues. To place your credit card order, subscribe by calling 813-596-4966. Or send a check to Nicholas Direct, Inc., 19918 Gulf Blvd., #7, Indian Shores, FL 34635.

Self-Publishing Seminar information on request.

FREE ● FREE ● FREE ● FREE ● FREE

Ted Nicholas would like to send you a gift for buying this book. Receive a cassette tape of a 90-minute interview with Ted Nicholas absolutely free conducted by famous author, Dr. Gary North, entitled "How To Turn Failure into Success." Write, call or fax your name and address now with words "please send free cassette tape," to Nicholas Direct, Inc., 19918 Gulf Blvd. #7, Indian Shores, FL 34635. Telephone: 813-596-4966, fax: 813-596-6900 (24 hours a day, 7 days a week).